The Self Starting Entrepreneurs Handbook

By T. L. Allen

Table of Contents

What Is an Entrepreneur?

An entrepreneur is a person who organizes a business and a person who likes to win at everything they do, by taking the risk of investing your hard earned money to make more money. Entrepreneurs exhibit confidence in themselves, and are very optimistic, they are disciplined self starter, why does an entrepreneur take these risks? The answer is clear for the money & they love what they do, they eat, breathe and sleep business. There are numerous benefits to being an entrepreneur, one of those benefits is you get to make your own decisions and don't have to answer to anyone, in other words you're your own boss. This is one of the things that make being an entrepreneur difficult because that means it would be left up to you 100% to make the business work and be a success. Being and training your-self to be a real risk taker is just one of the qualities an entrepreneur possesses, good negotiating skills are another skill an entrepreneur possess, good planning skills are a must failure to plan is definitely a plan that will fail. A successful entrepreneur takes out the time to plan his or her business ventures before even thinking about executing that plan into action, a planned strategy is king entrepreneurs are always negotiating not only with potential customers who might become lifelong customers, but also with people who are key elements to their business their hired staff. Being a successful negotiator means you are responsible for and to always come up with a solution where everyone comes out on top. As a business begins to grow, it becomes increasingly impossible for an entrepreneur to work alone, you'll need to hire some people to help you carry out some of your business tasks. It pays to be an entrepreneur, mostly all self made millionaires are self employed and they prepared their minds to become the millionaire they always wanted to be. If you have a burning desire to be financially free and independent, you must also be prepared for disappointments and setback along the way this is normal. Don't let fear of the unknown stop you from achieving your dreams. Are you entrepreneur material? Do you have an intense passion and drive to finally flourish in your life and succeed at everything you plan as far as business is concerned? These are some of the primary motivators to most successful entrepreneurs, their goals are set high and when they attain their goals and dreams they will set their goals even higher. Rather than resisting change an entrepreneur has the ability to adjust to change like a chameleon, at all cost many entrepreneurs blossom with change. The best part about being your own boss is if you don't like something you can change it at any time, you make the rules to the game and pull all the strings.

What Is a Business Plan?

A business plan is a tool which helps entrepreneurs to plan their business. It is a written summary that describes important aspect of the business you are planning. If you are planning on asking for funding to help you start your business a formal business plan will be needed. A written business plan helps with:

• It prevents mistakes when planning your business.

• It helps with identifying your strengths/ weaknesses/ and challenges that might lie ahead.

• It helps with spotting and correcting errors before they occur.

• It helps you communicate your ideas to lenders and future investors.

• It helps identify any other points or needs.

• Guides the start up of the business.

• Builds the entrepreneurs confidence.

• Helps redirect the entrepreneur to other points or ideas that may arise. These points will help you implement a variety of new ideas into a future business. Along with the other points you will find as you continue to read, if you wish to develop strategies for future success, it is necessary to gather the proper data and the solid information you'll need, this will give you a clear picture of what happens in other business similar to yours.

Naming Your New Business

Naming you business is extremely important, even though picking one can be stressful, you may actually have a number of different names lined up associated with your business not only should you pick a name that reflects your brand identity, but you should also ensure that the name you pick is properly registered. The number and types of names depend on the type of business you are planning on running. A strong name should be simple if you make it easy to spell and simple for starters, you should also give a thought to whether the name you pick is web ready, is the domain name even available?. Don't copy another business name. You should be able to sum up the basic objectives of your company in just a few sentences. If yours is a brand new business try considering a name that meets your current needs. If you are planning a business where most of your customers know you because they know about you and your reputation, you might want to use your own name.

• How will the name look? On the website or as a part of a logo or on your social media page

• What connotations does it invoke? Is your name too corporate or not corporate enough? Does it reflect your philosophy and culture? Does it appeal to your market?

• Is your business name unique? Pick a name that hasn't been claimed by others online or offline a quick web search and domain name search will alert you to any existing use.

• Trademarks- Check the trademark because trademark infringement can carry a high cost, before you pick a name check the U.S. patent and trademark office's website trademark search tool to see if a similar name exist.

• If you intend to incorporate your business, you'll need to contact your state whether your intended business name has already been claimed or is in use if you find a business operating under your supposed name, you may still be able to use it. Provided your business and the existing business offer different goods and services or are located in different regions.

• Pick a name that is web ready in order to pick a website address or URL, your business name needs to be unique and available. It should also be rich in key words that reflect what your business does, to find out if your business name has been claimed do a simple web search to see anybody is already using that name.

• Claim your social media identity, it is a good idea to claim your social media name early in the naming process even if you're not sure which site you intend to use. A name for your Face book page can be set up and changed, but you can only claim a vanity URL or a custom URL once you got 25 fans or likes. How to Registering Your Business Name Registering your business name is a confusing area for most new business owners. What does it mean? And what are you required to do? Registering your business name requires a process known as "Doing Business As (DBA)" name or trade name. This process shouldn't be confused with incorporation and it doesn't provide trademark protection, registering you "Doing Business As' name is simply the process of letting your state government know that you are doing as a business name other than your personal name or legal name of your partners or incorporation. If you are operating under your own personal name, then you can skip the process. If you establish your business as a sole proprietorship, you won't need to register your business at the state level; however, many states require sole proprietors to use their own name for the business name unless they formally file a different name. This is known as doing your business as (DBA) trade name, or a fictitious name.

Obtaining a Business License

Whether you are just starting out in business, No matter what kind of business you're interested in opening or starting a business license must be obtained. The Department of Finance representatives can assist you in registering your business and completing your business license application, please note that even independent contractors, self employed individuals, businesses with no employees, and part time businesses may also be subject to a license. As a business owner in whatever city you're operating you may also be subject to various taxes such as a business professional and occupational license (BPOL) or the business personal property taxes, the (BPOL) tax is generally based upon gross receipts, this may depend on the business classification. Example: A distributor might be a wholesaler and retailer so the business would be required to purchase a separate license for each business class. Whatever city you decide to open your new venture the City's Finance Department can assist you in determining tax type or types and amounts during the business application process. A business license can generally be obtained immediately after.

• General Business License- A license is issued to businesses with a physical location within the city limits. There is a fee for a general business license, the license is nontransferable.

• Home Businesses- Running a business from home is a very attractive idea for many entrepreneurs, but it is extremely important for home business operators to remember that they are conducting a business in a home which is most likely surrounded by other homes in a residential area. The city places certain restriction on the operation of home businesses to protect residents; nature of the neighborhood and prevent nuisance complaints regarding noise, dust and traffic, these rules protect you and your neighborhood. It's important for you as a home business operator to check all zoning codes, ordinances for the operation of your home business.

• Solicitors Permit- Every person who sells, solicit or takes orders for goods, wares, merchandise, books, subscriptions, photographs or services from private residence shall pay an annual license fee for a solicitors license.

Employee Permits (Must apply in person at city hall) Employee permits are based on a character review of the employee of certain types of business such as: taxi driver, card dealers, ice cream vendors, massage therapist, etc. permits are approved by the police department the fee for this kind of permit are usually $75.00 and is an annual license. Obtaining a Sales Tax Number A tax number is required for all businesses that intend to operate within any given city. Businesses must register with the department of taxation, for all taxes that may apply to the operation of the business, including sales taxable goods. To register, you must complete a combined registration form. Employer I.D. Number (EINs) an employer identification number (EIN) is also known as a federal tax identification number and is used to identify a business. Generally all businesses need an EIN, you can apply in a number of ways, and it's also available online. This is a free service offered by the Internal Revenue Service.

What Is A Wholesaler?

A wholesaler sales goods and merchandise to retailers for re-sale, a wholesaler is sometimes called a distributor as well. A wholesaler acts as an agent or a broker in buying merchandise for or selling merchandise to persons or companies. It is the wholesaler's job to assemble, put together and or sort, and grade goods in large lots and re-distribute them into small lots. Here's a list of markets a wholesaler makes their goods available too, such as retail markets, industrial, commercial, and institutional markets. There are a large number of important functions that are served by a wholesaler. Retail stores and factories, this middle man quickly helps a factory to turn a profit by buying goods from it. Once those good are out the door the manufacturer does not have to be concerned about recouping the expenses of making them. A wholesaler does not actually buy the good from a manufacturer, although it does store them. The wholesaler gets contracts for purchase of the goods from retailers, and receives a commission. In turn sells the merchandise to retailers, thus making sure the space occupied by the goods is paid for as soon as they leave the storage warehouse. Whether you want to sell your merchandise online or from a retail store outlet, if you're not manufacturing the products yourself you'll have to get your products from a wholesaler. The wholesaler being the mediator between the manufacturer's of the product and other businesses, by being allowed to buy the product from the manufacturer at a low price usually by discount base or based on volume buying, a wholesaler on the other hand may be able to buy 50,000 telephones a month for $4.00 each meaning he can then make a nice profit selling the phone for $10.00 a piece retail, which means you'll make a profit of $6.00 for each phone sold.

Retailers and wholesalers don't make a profit based on what they pay for a product and what they sell it for.

Wholesalers and manufactures may choose to deal only with businesses that are able to buy particular volumes of merchandise, or sign contracts to supply goods for a definite period of time. Some may not be willing to ship products to other countries. And wholesalers don't just sell products on; besides breaking products down into smaller units which can then be sold more conveniently to different retailers. The wholesaler may also assemble the goods as a part of the wholesale process. While the most common type of wholesaler is between the wholesaler and manufacturer and the retailer, an increasing number of wholesalers sell to other wholesalers. A wholesaler may also sale material to make goods, buy them from one manufacturer and then turn around and sell them to another.

• Getting into the wholesale business requires a lot of capital

• Storage is one of the primary functions in wholesaling.

• Manufactures are willing to give wholesalers better prices. It's easy to find a wholesale supplier if you know exactly what product you need. If you're just starting out and don't know exactly what you want to sell yet, if you do know what you want to sell, then below you will find the tips you need to help you on this path. You will also find a list of wholesalers, and manufacturers of products that you may find are suitable for you to start your new business enterprise.

• Manufacturers- There are some products you can buy directly from the manufacturer, this is what 'Boutique" stores do

• Importers- In some industries, a company may have exclusive rights to import and distribute a product in a certain country, some may sell directly to retailers, but more often they'll set up or sell to small local wholesalers

• Wholesaler- There are usually regional wholesalers who take delivery to boxcars sized lots, break them down, and sell truck load boxes of products to local wholesalers.

• Jobbers- "wagon peddlers" these are the guys who make daily deliveries to local grocers, and retail brick and mortar stores. Each product industry has its own unique distribution channels. Some retailers will move enough volume to bypass jobbers or maybe in a smaller industry, importers sell directly to retailers. When you first start you'll be buying from the smaller wholesalers at higher prices, as your volume increases, you'll be able to get better pricing and or move up the supply ladder to a bigger wholesaler. Take a list of wholesale distributors you get from the manufacturers and start contacting each one, what you're looking for are minimum order requirements and their wholesale unit prices., to get the best response be honest about what you're looking for, and keep your inquiries short and to the point. Before even considering buying wholesale merchandise for your store, visit one of your competitor's or a store selling the same merchandise you plan on selling in your store or online or flea market booth, browse the store's product selection make a mental note of the brands they carry, what product seems to be selling well? Which items are in the clearance bins? A retailer can often times find a product to sell in their stores by searching online, joining buying groups, using library resources, and the Thomas Register, also by attending trade shows, a trade show is one of the best places to buy wholesale merchandise for your store. A retailer can find many suppliers there, serving the same market, and their product offerings. Conduct an online search for trade shows or buyers' markets. Trade shows aren't often open to the general public so be prepared to show proof that you're an established business such as a resale certificate, tax I.D a business card or some other form of licensing or permit.

The Business of Manufacturers

Some manufacturers will sell their products at wholesale prices directly to the retailer, if they do; they may sell their product in large quaintly or at a high minimum order, if you have a particular product you want to sell, contact the manufacturer and ask them if they sell directly to dealers. If not, ask which distributor they sell their products through so you will know where to buy the items. When planning a successful business venture the supply and distributing channels are strictly critical, whether your company is a large operation producing handmade jewelry or DVD's there will be manufacturing concerns for all companies have them. The key to success when dealing with manufacturing concerns is to keep the inventory cost as low as possible. Manufacturing is when you take raw material and fabricate them into a finished product, producing goods in a viable constant stream over and over again; generally the continuous production reduces the cost of each unit. In order to maintain production and meet demand the goal would be to keep the inventory as low as possible, a part of manufacturing good by working very closely with your suppliers for the delivery of your goods, Distributors When planning a successful business venture the supply and distribution channels can be critical. A distributor usually sells a large variety of a certain classification of products. They must make a profit too, so their prices may be slightly higher than if the item was purchased directly from a manufacturer. A retailer can buy a lower quantity with little or no minimum order; some even offer free freight on orders over a certain amount. Once your store is open and doing business it will be easy to find a wholesaler or a distributor because the suppliers will be coming to you, instead of you looking for them. Importers Due to globalization importing products from another country is easier than it used to be, retailers can purchase products directly from importers, or buy the product from a foreign company. Before using this type of supplier, do your homework. It is important to understand all the aspects of the paperwork involved, shipping time, product life cycle, and all cost involved. In search for product at wholesale prices, you may find a wholesaler that don't just sell what you're looking for, but sell many types of merchandise. Some may sell closeouts, truckloads, pallets of merchandise, and even damaged goods, before buying wholesale merchandise from this kind of supplier, make sure you completely understand the conditions, prices and condition of the sale. Once you have located several sources of products, evaluate each vendor on a variety of factors, In order to bring the best quality merchandise to your customers. You'll need to buy from someone who will offer you quality products, reliable delivery, and superior customer service, below you will find a list of other factors to consider.

Stability, Price, Location, Shipping Options, Shipping Cost Customer Service, Terms of Sale, Returned Merchandise

Marketing Your Business by Word of Mouth

Once you build a great rapport with your current customers, make sure they appreciate your referrals; you could even offer them a referral bonus when they successfully spread the word about your business through word of mouth advertising. Don't forget to join the chamber of commerce and other organizations.

Creating a Marketing Strategy

A marketing strategy identifies customer groups which a particular business can better serve than its target competitors, and tailor product offerings, prices, distribution, promotional efforts and service. The strategy should address unmet customer needs that offer potential profitability. A good strategy helps a business focus on the target markets, it can serve best. By focusing your efforts on one or a few key marketing segments you'll reap the most from small investments. There are two methods used to segment a market.

• Geographic Segmentation- This segment serves as specializing in serving the needs of customers in a specific geographic area or location.

• Customer Segmentation- This identifies those customers that are most likely to buy the product and service and targeting those groups. Managing the Marketing Mix: Every marketing program has at least four key elements

• Product & Service- This includes concentrating on a narrow product line, developing a highly specialized product or service or providing a product service package containing unusually high quality service

• Promotion- promotion strategies focus on advertising and direct customer's interaction. It essential that you possess good salesmanship as a small business owner because of your business limited advertising budget. If you decide to market your products online this a cheap, quick and easy way to assure that your business receive high visibility.

• Price- When it comes to minimizing total revenue, it's crucial that you have the right price for your product and or service. High price means lower volume & visa versa. Smaller business can get away with asking for high prices for their product and service only because you're offering a personalized service.

• Distribution- The manufacture & wholesaler must determine how they want to distribute their products; small retailers should always consider cost and traffic flow in site selections, only because advertising and rent can be quite high, low cost, low traffic locations will definably mean spending more money on advertising in order for your business to build traffic.

Marketing Your Business

Marketing your business can include anything from getting your product ideas off a sketch pad and into the hands of your potential customers. Marketing includes act ivies such as

• Design a product that appears to be desirable to your customers.

• Perform marketing research and pricing.

• Promote your product and service through public relations, advertising, marketing, communication, sales and distribution. Incorporate Marketing into Your Business

• Engage yourself in at least one marketing activity every day.

• Determine how much gross income you would like to invest annually in marketing. • Set marketing goals every year.

• Promote your business at all times by carrying business cards.

• Publish a newsletter for your customers and potential customers.

• Develop an online brochure.

• Create a poster or calendar to give away to customers or potential customers

• Print a slogan or a lone line description on a letterhead, fax, cover sheet, or invoice.

• Get your business out on the internet.

• Create signature files to be used for all email messages; it should contain all your contact information, website address, and key information about your business that makes readers want to contact you.

• Announce free and special promotions at your contact pieces and don't forget to include the special promotions in the beginning of your letter or even outside the envelope. Marketing Your Business Using Apps Small business is now using apps to market their small business in this market is exploding like crazy. Mobile apps are one of the latest trends. Knowing how to use this trend is easy money. This is how it works: You may have an iphone, android, or other mobile devices that enable you to download "Apps' there are now hundreds of thousands of apps on the market and millions of people around the world using them. What you can do as a small business owner is to create your own killer app for mobile phone users.

• Promote your business

• Improve your customer service

• Get free advertising

• Increase customer loyalty there are many small businesses that are already doing these creating apps that do things for instance like giving the customer a copy of their menu on their phone, other businesses create fun games that feature their brand or provide something else of value to their customers. The idea is to create something that your customers would like to have on their phone and include your marketing information with it, coupons, special offers; calls to action are all must haves for making your app a success. The more value you are able to provide to users through your app, the more successful it will be. The more benefit and advantages you can provide to your customers through your app, the more of them will use it. Your app is only useful if people use it, people will only use your app if they have a good reason to.

• Create an app that users will love.

• Include your marketing plan and your call for action on your app.

• Encourage as many people as possible to download your app to their mobile devices.

• Your business could get sales and customers by creating valuable apps that people download.

• Promote your business with your app. Get Ready to Advertise what is the general purpose of your advertising? You'll need to focus on advertising routes, set measurable goals, so you can evaluate the success of your advertising campaign. Exactly how much can your small business afford to invest in advertising? Just remember this that what amounts you decide to invest will never seem like enough. If you give your income, expenses and sales projections simple addition and subtraction this will help you in determining how much you can afford to invest in advertising and promoting your business. Some businesses will go as far to invest 10% of their gross income on advertising, others just one percent. Put in the time to research to see what work best for your new small business, there are many sources of information out there to help you in your research. Your next mission will be to determine with advertising vehicle you will use to carry your message in the most effective way possible. Try to use as many of the below advertising tools as possible. Advertising Your Small Business If you want to grow a customer base quickly advertising is definitely the key. Advertising your new small business can be accomplished in a variety of methods. Successful promotion of your product and service requires careful planning in order to reach your target market and attract new customers.

• Advertise during the peak season for your business.

• Get a memorable phone number.

• Obtain a memorable URL or email address doesn't forget to include them on all marketing material.

• Promote your business jointly with other professionals.

• Advertise in a specialty directory or yellow pages.

• Write an ad in another language to read non English speaking customers, place ads in papers that cater to non English speaking community.

• Distribute advertising specialty products such as pens, mugs, magnets, etc...

• Create a direct mailing list of hot prospects.

• Also consider nontraditional ways of advertising such as billboards, bus backs, and popular websites.

• Consider placing ads in the classified section of the news paper The Basics of Advertising Your Business You just opened your new small retail shop; unfortunately no one is going to know about it until you use the basic tool to advertise. If advertising is done correctly, it can work wonders for your new small business, below you will find a list of the can do's and cannot do of small business advertising.

• Never forget to remind your customers about the benefits of your product or service.

• Create and establish your distinctive identity.

• Enhance your small business reputation.

• Encourage your customers to buy more of your product or service.

• Always look for ways to attract new customers

• Slowly build sales to boost your bottom line.

• Promote your business to customers, investors and others.

Business Ideas You Can Start

Developing a brand new business enterprise doesn't have to be hard. There are thousands of businesses you could start for under $1000.00; below you will find a list of some of those businesses. You are the only person who know exactly what kind of business you want to start, no one could answer that question for you., First of all what are you good at? This is the very first question to ask your-self before coming to a conclusion. What are you passionate about? When is a good time to start that new business venture you always dreamt about? The only way to answer any of the above questions would be to know what your goals are; the best way to find that out would be to make a list of your dreams, goals, and expectations. So, let's get started looking at those business prospects that can be built into the empire you always dreamt of running.

1) Online Advertising Directory- A business like this is very straight forward, you would start by advertising a website that features various information about rates, contact information, and any special promotion or discounts in terms of advertising rates, potential customer like business owners would visit the site and locate exactly the type of advertising they're interested in- that suit their marketing program and budget. Money is made by charging the advertising companies a fee to be listed on your website, as well as selling banner advertisements.

2) Charity events- Starting a business where you can start an advertising business that help local charities funding, all while building a very profitable business for yourself. Perhaps you could start a business helping local charities organize community charity events. Like community yard sales, golf tournaments, bake and arts and craft events. The charity would receive all admission fees for the event, while you will retain advertising revenues generated., by selling advertisement space as well as promotional items such as event t-shirts, and hats etc... The key to this kind of business is to build alliances with well recognized charities in your community or nearby communities. Just make sure the event is well promoted.

3) Window Displays- In the world of retail sale an elaborate window design is everything, this is one way to draw customers into the stores, and window displays attract the attention of passing customers. Starting a business that specialize in creating effective window displays for retail merchants , marketing a window display service can be as easy as approaching retail merchants and initially providing your service for free until the owner of the business realizes the benefits and increase in sales, that a well designed window display can garner. The free window display that you create can be used as a powerful marketing tool to present to other retail owners, placing a sign near the display that explains your service Along with contact information will help with the networking aspects of this new business of yours.

4) Door hanger Service- There are thousands of renovation and home service companies missing out on a very effective and extremely low cost advertising method for their business, and you can capitalize financially by introducing them to this advertising medium by starting your own door hanging design and delivery service. Door hangings are simply a type of marketing brochure that has been designed to fit on an entrance door handle. , what makes door hanging such an effective advertising tool is the fact that door hangers are noticed as people enter their homes, additionally door hangers can also act as a discount coupon with a company advertising message printed on the front and a coupon or special promotion printed on the back. Currently delivery rates are in the range of 25 to 30 cents per door hanger delivered, plus design and printing cost.

5) Promotional Products- Billions of dollars are spent in North America on promotional items such as t-shirts, pens, hats, and calendars by companies that give these promotional l items away to existing and potential clients of their business. Securing just a small portion of this very lucrative business marketing industry is not to manufacture and print the promotional items yourself, but to simply market these items and enlist the services of existing manufactures and printers to fulfill the orders. This is a business that requires excellent sales and marketing abilities and this business opportunity is not suitable for an individual who is scared to go out and ask for business. Aim to achieve yearly sales of $300,000 while maintain a 50% markup on all products sold, and the end result will be a home based advertising business that generates a pre tax and expense earnings of 100,000

6) Human Billboards- Human billboards advertise everything from new home development of car dealerships, to a new store opening on in the community. This is starting to catch on as a highly effective business advertising tool advertising and promoting your business and services. Human billboards are simply people that hold or wear signs or carry banners loaded down with promotional and advertising messages in high traffic areas of the community, usually outside in the front or in close proximity to the business they are promoting. The object of the human billboard is twofold, first get the attention of passing motorist and pedestrians, and once you have their attention get them to take action. This simply means you want these people to go to the business that is being promoted. There are really two types of aspects of operating this type of business marketing and the people who will be the human billboards. Seek to hire homemakers, students, actors, musicians, and retirees basically anyone that is available to work on a short training program; vital to the success of the business will be the ability of the human billboards to get the desired response. Which of course is to be noticed, the training program can be focused on body language and vocal phrasing, and both which if used correctly can be highly effective.

7) Vehicle Advertising- Ever see a car or truck driving around with an advertisement on it? You could be the party responsible for getting that ad on that vehicle, provided of course, the vehicle slows down just long enough for you to place the ad there is money to be made and you will serve as the middle man or woman. Finding interested advertisers and suitable vehicles. There are also trucks that drive around exclusively for the purpose of carrying a large billboard ad, this can be a bit more costly as you would need to own or lease a truck.

8) Calendars- Thousands of businesses give out promotional calendars to clients and vendors as an excellent low cost start up business is putting together calendars especially for clients. Pictures can be included from the client, from photographers or even from outside sources with the permission of the photographer of course, other forms of art and electronic graphics can also be an option, you bill the client for putting together the calendar and handling layout and printing. You can also make money by selling advertising space to various businesses to advertise for a calendar and to supply you with graphic artwork. The advertisers will pay to be included in the calendar and you then

9) Advertising Agency- All it takes to start in the advertising business is creativity, and some marketing abilities, advertising agencies create the ad images, and the right look and feel, that will help their clients sell their products and service to the public. Copyrights and graphic artist are the two key elements to making it work, and if you have one of those key elements this would be your great starting point. A good media planner will decide which are the right promotional avenues for each one of your clients, and potential clients and how they will effectively position themselves, and finally you will need someone to run the business aspect of the agency by paying the bills, ordering the supplies, invoicing clients, and balancing the budget. Whether you serve as a one person, creative, production, and financial wiz or find a few key people to help launch the business from your basement or from the attic, an advertising agency can start off with just a hand full of clients and build into an empire.

10) Custom Airbrushing- Airbrush painting is very popular and has many uses, including customizing cars, creating wall murals, decorating clothes, and creating a one of a kind paint finish on almost any product. The equipment necessary for this type of business is inexpensive and can be ordered through art supply or paint supply stores. The charge to create custom airbrushed images was $60.00 per hour plus material with no guaranteed on how long it would take to finish the job. Working a mere 25 hours a week provides airbrushing services can earn you as much as $70,000 per year.

11) Native American Art- Native American people create some of the most beautiful art in the world, and these artworks are high in demand especially in overseas markets such as Japan, Germany and the United Kingdom. The demand for Native Art creates a great business opportunity for you if you have a good contact base in foreign countries. This business allows you to work as a highly compensated broker by representing native artist locally, and use your international contacts to set up distribution channels in foreign countries. The business can work in reverse, you can start up distribution channels in North America representing artist from foreign countries. This business does require a lot of research and set up time, but the potential rewards can justify the effort.

12) Mobile Art Gallery- Art is big business, and starting a mobile art gallery can put you on the road to riches, take a traditional art gallery, place wheels on it and you have this business opportunity in a nutshell. In this business, you will want to work with hundreds of artist or more, this is a volume based

operation. Once you have selected the artist, begin to establish locations where the art work will be featured. Good locations include doctors' offices, waiting rooms, office lobbies, restaurants, shopping malls, hospitals, and all high traffic gathering places, the art can be displayed in these locations with a small place card on each piece, when a potential customer calls to inquire about a particular piece of art for sale, you would simply sell the art over the phone and arrange a delivery to the purchaser. If a piece of art sells for $100.00 then you would give the artist $50.00 the host location $10.00 and keep $40.00 for yourself, as you can see on a volume basis there enormous potential for profit, image if you had only 100 locations selling just two pieces of art per month at an average sale price of $150.00 you would stand to make more than $10,000 a month

13) Hand Painted Greeting Cards- This is a very large market demand for hand painted greeting cards and post cards, if you have the talent to do this yourself that great, but if not there are hundreds of artist who will be glad to assist you for a fee. The greeting cards and postcards can be wholesaled to retailers or sold directly to companies to give as corporate gifts to clients, if you plan on specializing in hand painted greeting cards you will want to sell them in high traffic tourist areas like airports, tourist attractions, and beaches, whatever you decide to do this business can be very profitable and fun, and best of all it can be started from peanuts. Using some digital photographs of your work, you can easily market greeting cards, or calendars for that matter on websites, whether it is your own site or on the sites of other online businesses, but they may want to take a percentage of the profits, they also can provide you with great exposure.

14) Mirror Art- Mirror art is simple, small pieces of mirror in various shapes and colors that has been assembled to resemble a picture, landscape or even abstract designs, mirror art is becoming very trendy for use at home decorations in most cases a trip to the mirror shop will result in all the mirror you will need for this new business venture and usually at no cost. Most glass shops dispose of mirror cutoff pieces that are too small to sell, but those same pieces of mirror are perfect sized to create mirror art. The equipment needed to create the art is inexpensive and includes a few hand tools and a glass grinder. Also patterns are available to make the mirror art or you can create your own. Once the job is completed, the art can be sold via flea market booths, or on a website or to interior decorators and designers.

15) Cartoonist- If you have a knack for drawing you can serve as a commercial cartoonist for any kind of publishing or advertising to market your skills. You'll need to put together a portfolio of your best work and set up appointments to meet editorial directors, publishers, editors, writers or and directors, any of whom may need your services. Most cartoonist's work on their own meaning, you will create the message behind the cartoon yourself, while others may team with someone else who come up with the concept, the captions, or both. Good cartoonist working for major newspapers can make upwards of $70,000 annually, while freelancers can do well if they establish a niche and work regularly for several clients.

16) Book Illustrators- If you love to draw put together a portfolio of book covers and Illustrations for non existing books, or even your visions for existing books. These will serve as samples for you to show clients, who will include book publishers, book packagers, agents, and authors, any of whom can hire you to illustrate forthcoming books. You may want to specialize in a particular area such as children's books; royalties are typically 50/50 split with the author as is also the case with the advance. A Illustrator who is hired to do x number of drawings for fiction or nonfiction books may be paid per Illustration which will be determined by the market for the type of books, the size of the publishing house and other factors.

17) Fashion Illustrator- Specializing in this industry can make it easy to get work because you will be mastering specific skills, in some cases, depending on the specialty there is less competition. There are many possible avenues for which you can seek work if you have the technical and drawing skills, plus a good eye for details, you can draw the fashion and their many accessories, hats clothes, handbags etc... periodically retail stores, advertising agencies, department stores, catalog galleries and designers just to name a few of the possibilities. As with a career in visual art you will need to have a portfolio book, the CD –Rom version, and a website that you can direct people to four samples. Most often you can run your career as a fashion Illustrator from your home office, or studio. Start up cost are minimal and if you are good, there is a tremendous upside to this business, depending on how well you market yourself

. 18) Day Care Center- Day care is a booming industry simply due to the fact that most families today require full time incomes, just to survive financially. There are various types of day care centers such as home based, store front, mall and business locations and mobile daycare centers. And all of them have their benefits and drawbacks. Once you have determined the operation, location and type of day care center, the next step will be to bring in the parents with their children, this can be accomplished in many ways, and a good way to do that is with a strong marketing presentation. Parents want to know that their children will be safe, happy and well cared for as well as mentally stimulated while their away at work, Home based day care faculties can cost as little as $5,000 dollar to establish, while full scale day care centers operated from an independent business location can cost as much as $100,000 to start, of course there are zoning laws may force you to put the brakes on a home based day care center., once you have established the kind of day care center you want to establish, the next step would be to factor in all overhead cost and an established cost per child to provide your service, you will then add a markup or profit margin onto this cost to establish as retail cost., regardless of the size or type of service you provide, you can expect a healthy return on your investment. You should have no difficulty earning in excess of $40,000 per year

19) Children's Party Service- Everyday thousands of children has birthday parties, graduations, or they just deserve to have a little fun. The main consideration for starting this type of business a party service is whether the business will be operated from a fixed location or on a mobile basis. Once you have established the base of operation, you can begin to market

the party service. A great starting point would be to design colorful brochures describing your service, set up a website with prices and various party themes. Tap into what today's kids are interested in and then creating themes for that age group, offer a variety of well planned two hour party packages and make the party service a one stop shopping experience, which includes a choice of party favors, cakes, and other foods as well, it's not a bad idea to include some educational value too. If you do set up a fixed location from which to hold the parties, you will definitely need to look into establishing some liability insurance before opening your doors. Then set up the space to be child friendly, see if you can find a place with plenty of space, good lightening, few stairs, and ample parking before opening a party zone so to speak.

20) Educational Toy's- Educational toys and games will always be in popular demand , you can design and develop the toy and games yourself or act as an agent for manufacturing, both methods can be a very profitable way to earn an income and be self employed. There are various approaches to marketing educational toys and games, this includes the internet, mail order, home parties, flea markets, and sells to specialty retailers on a wholesale basis. A unique marketing method may be to hold free seminars for parents with a central theme, perhaps "improve your child's reading skills" the seminar would state all the facts and benefits that improve reading comprehension has for their children. During the free seminar you would promote the product you want parents to purchase at the conclusion. If you decide to choose this route to promote your toys and games, be sure to establish an alliance with child educational experts to speak at the seminar on the subject of the benefits of educational children's toys and games.

21) Coloring Books- To personalize children coloring books the equipment required and approach to marketing are very similar, to that of the story book venture, however an additional marketing technique that can be employed is to design a retail sales kiosk and located the kiosk in a busy mall on the weekends, this kind of retail location will enable you to personalize and sell the coloring books on the site. Do not limit your ability to generate revenue, with the right software, you can also produce children's u-color it posters, restaurant place mats, and even specialty greeting cards, all of which can also be sold via sales kiosk, as well as flea markets and fairs to increase your revenues and profits.

22) Children Used Clothing Sale- Most children's clothing is expensive, you can open a store or rent a booth at the flea market and at fairs and sale second hand clothing, and which case you can purchase good quality second hand children's clothing at bargain basement prices and resell the clothing for a profit accepting consignment clothing is one way to reduce business startup cost. The garments will need to be washed prior the business sale of them be sure you have cataloged or know the web address of leading retailers so that you can properly estimate the value of the clothing you will be purchasing for resale purposes. If you decide to operate from retail store locations you will need about $25,000 to purchase equipment, and start stocking, and operate the business. If you choose the route of the weekend flea market the business startup cost will be greatly reduced and you could get started for less than $3,000 initial investment. To be profitable in this type of retail venture, try to maintain a 100% markup on clothing items you purchase for resale. And always charge 40 to

50% commission for any consignments you accept and sell. If you can maintain yearly gross sales of $100,000 you should have no problems netting $30,000 a year after expenses. If the business is operating from a fixed location you can add additional revenue from renting children's costumes, there will be a onetime expense to purchase the costumes.

23) Used Baby Equipment- Baby equipment such as strollers, car seats, and cribs are very expensive these days, so why not start your own business that specializes in clean good quality second hand equipment for babies? This kind of business can be started for less than $15,000, and can be operated from a small retail location or from your home. You can purchase item from parents and mark them up by at least 100 percent for resale purposes depending on the item. You can also take in items on a consignment basis to reduce business start up cost. A business like this is suited for a person with a number of contacts with parents in your community. Additional income and profits can also be earned by adding a cloth diaper delivery service. If your business specializes in used products, always refer to your merchandise as refurbished or renewed, this will give your business a more professional appearance and even allow you to charge a premium for your refurbished merchandise.

24) Talent Agent for Kids- Are you searching for a low income business home based business opportunity? That has the potential to be lots of fun and very profitable, perhaps you should think about starting a talent agency for kids. This type of business enterprise is very easy to activate and there will be no shortage of potential clients, as children think about hamming it up for the camera, currently children agents are charging a commission rate between 10 to 20 percent of their clients earning. Many agents also represent children in the modeling profession as well as those involved in voice over work for radio

and television. To gain exposure to producers and directors for the business, you can start an e-mail newsletter to local production companies and theater groups, and a personal visit campaign promoting your talent

25) Work Uniforms- The first option is to establish a retail storefront location to stock and sell work uniforms, and the second option would be to establish a mobile business that sells work uniforms from a cube van or a delivery truck, both options have drawbacks and benefits in terms of the business, however the second option of being a retailer of working uniforms would be less costly to establish, as well as to operate on a monthly basis. This kind of uniform and work clothing that can be sold, including work overalls, health care uniforms, and school sportswear, Also stockings and specialized work footwear, such as steel toe work boots can earn additional revenue. Regardless if the business is operating from a fixed location or on a mobile basis. One of the main marketing tools required, will be designed and produce a full colored catalog and a website that feature the work wear available.

26) Used Wedding Gowns- Selling second hand wedding gowns from home as well as on the internet for a profit, in a nutshell, the main objective is to purchase second hand wedding gowns and accessories at a bargain basement price and resell them the gown for a profit. The gowns can be sold from a home base location as well as on the internet by developing your own website, in addition to purchasing gowns you can also accept consignment gowns and retain 25 to 40 % of the sales value for providing the service. For additional income you could also sell

veils, headpieces, garters, and other accessories both new and used, Advertise your business in the local newspaper and build alliances with wedding planners to promote the business.

28) Second Hand Clothing Store- Selling clothes through a consignment shop or resale shop can be a great business for someone who loves fashion merchandising and sales. There is a strong market for used clothing and other items. There are several options for selling used clothing, you could open a retail store as your storefront, or rent a booth or a table at the flea market. This method is a great income booster; there are a lot of ways to pursue this business. First you must decide where and how to get the used clothing, people could bring you there used clothes; you should have policies in place about the used clothing you will accept. Determine what kind of clothing you want to sell, either designer clothing, vintage clothing is all ideas of specialty items. You will need racks and hangers for hanging the clothing, shelves, display stands, and changing rooms, you will also need a check out area for the customers to purchase their items. Choose the best avenue to advertise your store via internet, fliers or display ad's in the local newspaper.

29) Pet Clothing- Starting a business that specializes in making clothing for pets, first you must be familiar with sketching designs, cutting patterns selecting appropriate material for your designs, there are a couple of approaches to establishing this kind of business, the first being design, manufacture, and marketing the pet clothing , as with any new business you must consider the advantages and disadvantages, the second approach would be purchase the clothing straight from a manufacture on a wholesale basis for resell purposes or have a

local seamstress design and manufacture the clothing for you. Products can be marketed in local pet stores, sold at flea markets, pet grooming salons, and fairs via flier handed to people who are out walking their dogs you can also set up a website and sell the product directly on line. The more unique your designs are, the more you can rely on word of mouth marketing.

30) Dry Clean Service- Owning and operating a dry clean, service can be very profitable. You will need to purchase the necessary permits, licenses, and insurance in order to run this type of business, operating your business legal is a major step in earning your customers' trust. The business location is very important because you cannot run a business like this from home. Dry cleaning requires specialty equipment, and you will need to invest in a variety of machines such as conveyors, laundry hot leads, foam finishers, shirt finishers, and other machine to accommodate all the clothing and household items brought to you daily. Your staff doesn't have to have experience in the dry cleaning service business, you may train them accordingly.

31) Cap Business- You will need to find wholesalers, and cap distributors, get insurance in the event in case someone steals from your store. Place an ad in the classified section of your local newspaper to find employees, Order your first batch of hats from your distributor, buy hat racks and display cases, purchase dummy displays to wear the caps you want displayed. Marketing through local newspapers and television as well as radio stations will get the word out fairly quick. Highlight the

best benefits of wearing your caps. Baseball style caps with the name of teams, towns or cities, even business logo's there are numerous cap styles and you can purchase most of your inventory for $5.00 or less, buy wholesale, and then sell caps at various prices starting at $10.00 and up.

32) Board Room Facilities and Business Center- The board room facility would have to be well equipped with office fixtures, furniture and other office equipment, such as a private meeting room, computer, a wireless internet connection, copiers, overhead projectors, multi line and function telephone system, stationery supplies, and other elated client support services and products. You will need access to a catering service, messenger service, and administrative office service. When choosing a location for this business the following should be considered, a central location, good parking, at least 1,500 square feet of floor space. Prior to establishing the business, a market study should indicate if the business would be supported mainly by home base business owners, or business travelers, in the latter case, a facility near an airport this could be very beneficial.

33) Custom Computer Sales- A business selling computer systems and equipment is a very competitive sector, the only you could go up against the numerous retailers and manufacturers who sell computer is to have the ability to build and sell customized computers for specific purposes, such as engineering, medical technology, and advance technical concerns, if you are smart enough to put the various components together for clients and build the models they need, you could charge several thousands of dollars for this kind

of specialized equipment. A business like this requires that you know the business inside out, as well as staying on top of the latest technology. You'll also need to offer top notch customer service.

34) Computer Upgrade Service- Starting a business that requires computer upgrading already existing equipment, is a great business that has great potential, a computer upgrade service is a very easy service to get rolling, provided that you have the skills, and equipment necessary to complete upgrading task, such as installing more memory into the hard drive, replace a hard drive, set up a wireless system, building onto an already existing network, or setting one up for a company from scratch, or add a new disk drive to an already existing system, in addition you should market yourself to the home based computer users, providing them business from a home base while providing clients with a mobile service is the best way to keep operating overhead minimum. Plus, you'll potentially increase the size of your target market.

35) Computer Cleaning Service- The fastest and efficient way to establish a computer cleaning service that specialize in cleaning computers used for business purposes, would be to establish an alliance with commercial office cleaners so that they can recommend your services to their clients. The only requirement for operating a computer cleaning service is to have the proper equipment to clean computers along with the needed skills and a liability insurance policy.

36) Used Computer Sales- Purchase secondhand computers and equipment from auctions and by way of surplus sales, and resell the equipment for a profit this is a terrific new home based business, Many corporations and government agencies, as well as educational facilities, upgrade and replace their computer equipment on a regular basis. Often times the equipment are only a few years old, and can be purchased at 5% less than the original purchase cost. Trick is to make sure the computer system is not too antique, and then sell it to individuals who are looking for second hand computers Local classified ads, fliers, posters, in busy locations flea markets, or local fairs are placed to market such a home based business.

37) Mobile Computer Training- Companies that have recently upgraded their computer systems or have introduced new software into the business require the students come to their business location for training classes. Computer upgrades, training or learn the benefits of new software programs, here lies the business opportunity, combining your computer, software, and marketing skills as well as your experience. You can start a mobile computer training service; the classes can be conducted at the client's location as well as using the client's computer equipment, income range at a least $50 bucks an hour.

38) Website Quality Consultant- As a website quality consultant, you can view your client's website and submit a full report to them, in exchange for $150.00 consultant fee give the business owner the real lowdown on the quality of their website, most small business owner forget that their website is a tool that will promote their business it provides quality information and

service. The report could include a comparison to competitor's sites, a rating on how user friendly site is, and suggestions on how the site could be improved such as practical tips for user friendly functionality and or a better design, you could show the business owner ways to provide enhanced visitor services. Improve the contents and graphics or navigating or all the above. The cost of this very beneficial consulting service is low, but the difference could mean cyber failure or cyber business success. This is how you could build your business y marketing the success of other business

39) Website Design- You could take crash courses at the local college on website designing, or you could hire someone who already knows how to design a website and concentrate all of your energy on marketing and promotion. There is a lot of competition when it comes to website design, you may want to take a more hands on approach an market your service in your own community and city, it's best to start by designing a few sample sites for your potential client's. One designed in an e-commerce format and one as an information portal, next initiate a telephone campaign and lots of letter writing to introduce yourself and your service to small business owners that currently do not have a business website. The whole point is to get presentation appointments at their place of business. Armed with your notebook or laptop computer, you can meet with business owners, present your sample sites and explain the benefits of your website design service.

40) Telecommunication Specialist- Being a telecommunications specialist can be a simple set up, telecommunication specialist design voice and data communications systems, supervise installation of these systems, and provide maintenance and service to clients after the installation process. By setting up wireless transmissions, voice transmissions, and data communication, as well as satellite communication all are a part of the duties of a telecommunication specialist. If you have high tech skills, this just may be the business for you, one you can stay on top of by staying ahead of the ever changing technical world. It's best to market yourselves to new businesses and growing businesses of all sizes. As a telecommunication specialist, you can charge a $100 plus per hour and work from a home base, although you will spend a majority of your time in home offices or satellite offices of larger businesses.

41) Woodcarving- woodcarvings sell like crazy, but they can also make you some money. In the right environment you could have a hot business to could make you lots of cash, sold in places like flea markets, craft shows, or specialty retail shops. Find a retailer that will stock the wood carvings for you in their store on consignment, because the owners of these businesses know how well wood carvings sell. If you want to keep a bulk of the profit for yourself, you can always sell your woodcarving straight to the consumer yourself. Or on your own website or by local advertisements featuring pictures of the woodcarvings, or you could sell them to an auction website like eBay.

42) Christmas Decorations- The secret to success when selling Christmas decorations is that your decoration you plan on selling must be unique and appealing. This new business enterprise is very straight forward and could be initiated by anyone. Simply design, produce and sell custom one of kind decorations, the decorations can be sold directly to retailers, on a wholesale basis or directly to consumers via renting a sales table at an art and craft show. While this is obviously a seasonal business, don't be fooled and wait too far into year to get started you should be ready to start selling in September and October at the latest.

43) Flower Arrangements- The opportunities for making money selling flower arrangements are endless, flowers are purchased daily for many occasions, and the flowers would have to be arranged once they are at whatever event you are to set them up for, everything from arranging small bouquets, to large center pieces or for interior decorations, and for event planners. You can also supply real estate agent with thank you flowers for their clients who have recently purchased a home. Gaining new clients for this business is very easy as you prepare samples of your work and hand delivering them to potential clients with a full marketing presentation outlining the value and benefits of your service, this is great part time home based business to set in motion a brand new way to earn substantial income yearly are unlimited.

44) Soap Making- Soap making is a personal item and therefore should be marketed on a personal level. If you decide to get into the soap making business, you could market your product to retail stores, flea markets, health shops, craft fairs, bath shops, There are thousands of books and website that will teach you how to hone your craft, However while many people find that homemade soap smells great and are also healthier for the skin few people take the time to make them. The scent is a big marketing plus, begins making soap for fun and for profit.

45) Specialty Greeting Cards- You could start a business that customizes business cards for clients it's a terrific business to set into action, In order to be successful in this business, you would need to offer a higher quality card and sell your ability to design and create something unique and original. In addition to high quality color printer you will also need a top of the line computer design software, all of your marketing efforts should be focused on potential customer as well as existing customers. Who would benefit the most form, sending customized greeting cards, give them some ideas of what you can design and do is unique and create the best greeting card each and every time you create one. Potential customers would include corporate associates, organization, professionals, and individual consumers who would be prepared to purchase the specialty cards in minimum orders of 50 at one time, potential income earnings range from $20 to $30 dollars an hour.

46) Company Newsletter- Design and print company newsletters salespersons and stockbrokers is a fantastic low income investment business, start that can generate a great income. Monthly news letter is a great way for salespeople and business owners to stay in contact with their clients, and promote monthly specials, ad this is a great way to generate new business. Many businesses still prefer a letter you can hold din your hand, rather than an electronic newsletter. The key is to show the company's that you have the ability to this for them; to succeed in this type of venture you will need the following.

47) Marketing Brochures- this business creates a great business opportunity for an entrepreneur with sales and marketing experience. By creating highly effective brochures for your clients, once again this type of business can be operated from your home o a part time or full time bases as the business grows. Potential clients can include just about any business that relies on marketing brochures, to generate some interest in their business, product and service your potential income would range from $35 dollars per hour. 48) Restaurant Menus- restaurants can be ideal clients to work with, due to the fact that menus regularly change and generate only a short production run, thus excluding many larger commercial printers, this type of desktop publishing business is ideally operated on a part time basis and it would require only and full of regular clients to produce a substantial part-time income. In addition to a computer, you will also need a color printer that can produce large menu pages, up to 11 inch by 17 inch, addition revenue can also be earned by creating ad producing restaurant paper place mats and menu describing daily specials.

49) Building History Guides- A building history guide can be published each month ad distributed free of charge throughout your community. This business can also be started from home on your desktop computer, if you are a fan of history you should think about writing a guide about local historical buildings. Revenues to support the business would be earned by selling advertising space in the guide to local merchants wishing to promote their products and service. Furthermore most of the locals can provide the historical information you're looking for and pictures featured in the guide. Thus reducing the time it will take to produce the monthly publication. Such an s guide will be very popular in areas known for their historical past. This type of guide can be sold through local realtors in exchange for a commission.

50) Business Form Templates- The purpose of this type of business is to sell business form templates which are simple blank business documents and forms in print format or on CD-ROM or floppy disk that has been specially designed to be used in particular business industries, such as automotive sales, manufacturing, or home renovation these forms make it easier for business owners to establish operating and record keeping systems for their businesses. The business form and documents can include items such as a monthly expense reports, work orders, purchase orders, sales receipts, bookkeeping forms, packing slips, sales reports, just to name a few. Business form templates can be packaged and sold to specialty retailers on a wholesale basis or directly to consumers via the website.

51) For Sale by Owner Kits- Millions of cars, boats, homes, and businesses are sold every day by private owners of these items, this makes for an exciting and creative business opportunity, you could start a desktop publishing business that specializes in for sale by owner marketing kits. This kit's can be created especially for the purpose of marketing one particular item, and offer to purchase and contract forms in template form. The kit's can be in print format or on CD-Rom and sold to retailers on a wholesale basis or directly to the consumer via mail order on the internet. Once you've established the profit potential for this type of business is outstanding and the market for the product in unlimited.

52) Small Business Guides- Starting a desk top publishing business in your community that specialize in creating a monthly small business guide is a terrific new business venture to set in motion, This small business guide can be distributed for free of charge to small and home based business owners throughout the community and supported by selling advertising space to local companies wishing to advertise their businesses and their product and service, and the guide also have information and articles featuring in the monthly guide can also include tips for improving the performance of a business, legal issues pertaining to business and other information small business owners need to know and find useful. You can also have people subscribe to an online version of the guide.

53) Commercial Real-Estate Guide- You could create a monthly publication that features commercial real-estate for sale, rent or lease; this is a great home based desktop publishing business to start. The paper could also include business and franchise opportunities advertisements. Securing revenue for this monthly paper can be accomplished in two ways, one being, is to charge consumers to purchase the paper through retail distribution, second being by selling the advertising space to agents and brokers. The key to do this successfully is for you to align with area brokers and agents making sure to update the listings as soon as new real estate becomes available.

54) School Calendars- This is a great part-time opportunity to make some extra income all you have to do is get in touch with the local school board in your area or in various areas and put together a calendar for the school year indicating days off, half days, special school events, report card time, graduation rehearsals, year book photos, graduation day, etc... you can also include school photos, most school districts have this information on hand in advance but often times they don't take the time to compile it on one year long calendar. Local advertisers can pay for the calendars if the schools are facing budgetary constraints.

55) Dunk Tank Rentals- A dunk tank rental does have a lot of benefits to be considered, including limited competition. It's a low start up investment, the ability to manage from a home based office, no inventory, and flexible business hours, minimal overhead, and this business also has great profit potential. Your potential customers would include sports associations, charities,

business associates, schools, fund raising consultants, special event planners, kid party planner's, caterers, as well as community organizations, fundraising charities will rent the tank in conjunction with a fundraising carnival, party or sports event, and then charge people in attendance with a fee o attempt to dunk the unfortunate soul who has been chosen to take the wet seat, what better way than a dunk tank to make money.

56) Used CD Music Shop- If you interested in starting a business venture in the fast paced music business, you could invest in a second hand musical compact discs. To operate business of this stature locations such as the flea market, local fairs, or jobbing putting your CD's or racks in stores, in order to get enough inventory to make your business work, place classified ads in the local newspaper offering to purchase whole and CD compacts collections, CD's ranging from $5 to $10 bucks and up.

57) Entertainment Hotline Service- To start a business as an entertainment hotline service that includes movie listings, community events, and concerts, fairs, carnivals, plays and whatever may be going in your community and surrounding areas, if you want to ad features, and other discount specials. Your income base would generate from charging fee's to companies as a monthly membership who would be interested in selecting spots on your entertainment hotline service.

58) Street Entertainer- If you are gifted with talent such as walking on stilts, juggling, or miming, etc…. start a business venture as a street entertainer this business just might be for you, many street entertainers can generate up to $1,000 a week. In a business like this location is everything, you will have to find a busy location in order to pull in this kind of capital. In some states a permit or license may be needed to conduct your performance, research is vital to assure that you don't get fined or even arrested. Performing at fairs, carnivals, or community fundraising events, or other gathering taking place in your community would be an avenue to explore, you may even find that grand opening celebration may hire you such as retail outlets, malls, hotels, or other established businesses.

59) Recording Studio- In order to open a recording studio you will definitely need capital, but the capital you invest in your studio the rewards you receive once your business is up and operating will be even greater. You could even start a business venture like this as a home based business, studios are for voice over's, radio advertising, compact disc recording, and video cassette recording, If you don't have experience in the recording industry, it would be wise do your research before even considering a business venture of this caliber. The income generated from your investment in a recording studio would exceed $100,000 a year plus profits after wages, and expenses and taxes.

60) Wedding Entertainer Booker- to start a wedding entertainer booking service for singers, bands, do's, and talented singers, you would instantly become a middle man or woman representing multiple talented wedding performers, as an agent you would retain a portion of the talent performance fee as your commission Profits ranging from $20,000 per year. You would need to come up with at least a dozen good singers and bands that are always on call to play or sing at weddings & than it would be up to you to market your groups and bands and singers and dj's to wedding planners, catering halls, bridal shops etc...

61) Red Carpet Service- The market for a service that supply park8ing valets, ushers, event planners, and professional emcee's, is huge profit business venture. When business owners host special events and weddings, tradeshows, or even political events, and award ceremonies, the profit potential will fluctuate. This is a word of mouth client referral business. However on a part time basis a business of this stature can generate up to $20,000 per year or even more depending on how many events you work.

62) Music Fest Promoter- This is a great opportunity and business to become a music Fest promoter. It would require a great amount of research to become a music Fest promoter, in order to get your foot in the door; you may want to organize a small local concert in your community in order to build up your reputation. By first deciding what kind of music you want to promote, Hip Hop, R&B, Jazz, Country, Rock and Roll, there are seven steps to start a business of this nature.

• Build up a relationship with co-sponsors for the event

• Look for a location such as parks, beaches, outside arena's, and stadiums

• Applying for the necessary permits

• Look for promoters and vendors to sponsor the event.

• Build up a volunteer work force to assist you in the event

• Print tickets

• Promotion is key online, newspapers, fliers, etc... 63) Alcohol Free Club- To start a business venture of this nature that doesn't serve alcoholic beverages in a society where people are starting to live healthier lifestyles, your benefits would include lower investment capital, lower liability premiums, as well as regulations, and less competition, you have better increase of term operating locations, a establishment like this could either serve adults, or teens up to 15 years of age safety would be the key in this well managed environment.

64) Voice Over's- To make it in a business of this nature, your voice would definitely have to your greatest asset. Your client base would include advertising agencies, film producers, radio commercials, radio stations, publishers of audio books as well as corporations for telephone messages. People who specialize in supplying their voice for this type of work charge fee's that range from $50 to $75 dollars an hour, As a union performer (National Performers Union) you could even earn up to $600 or more per job, you will need a very good demo tape which could cost you up to $500 to $2,000 dollars but that would an investment worth making in your career or business. Once you have this demo it would be wise to send it to agents.

65) Old Time Radio Programs- Radio programs from the 30's, 40's, 50's and 60's era are becoming popular once again. If you go into a business of this nature, try to purchase the rights to re-record old time radio programs onto compact disc. Once the process is complete the CD"s can be sold to retailers on a wholesale basis, or directly to consumers on a mail-order basis, by advertising in the newspapers or by way of magazine the profits from this business venture could be outstanding, considering it only cost a couple of dollars to mass produce the CD's.

66) Short Run CD Rom Production- Producing compact disc for clients is a very unique business venture, by providing your service to clients with a short run compact disc service production; this service is huge and growing by the second. Start up cost of the business is high, but once your business is established. The profits will be greater.

67) Entertainment Booking Agent- Starting a business as a freelance entertainment booking agent, you will be actively booking entertainers into venues and singers, bands, theater productions, and other performers in shows, clubs, films, and so on. The key to success is your contacts and you will need a Rolodex of very good ones. Your first thing to do would be to look into who would be willing to hire your entertainers, party planners, club owners, etc.... the second would be to have a list of best performers with demo's DVD's, resumes, Bio's and head shots, as a entertainment booking agent you are responsible for working out deals and details between the venue management and the performers. Once an alliance is built with the entertainers you will retain a portion of their fee's which is the talent receives. Get familiar with current rates this is where extensive research comes in.

68) Disc Jockey Service- DJ's service is high in demand, there are four success elements required in order to start a business venture of this nature.

• You must have an excellent music selection

• You must possess top notch dj equipment

• You must have a talent for speaking and an outgoing personality

• Marketing Skills Once you have established all of the above your potential clients would be wedding planners, event planners, tour operators, night club owners, individuals seeking your services as a disc jockey for graduation celebrations, and other events such as sweet sixteen parties, bar Mitzvahs, DJ's with full packages of one or five dancers, give away items, video screen, and various other items. The potential earnings for a vent garner $1,000 or $6,000 for a single party, two parties per weekend at $3,000 each would generate over $300,000 per year if you are good, word of mouth advertising would make it almost necessary to spend money on marketing.

69) Band Manager- It would be best to start a business of this stature on a part time basis, as a home based business whole representing at least two musical bands or a solo musical performer. Or run a full time management, agency that represents multiple talents. Both approaches to establish such an operation you would have to determine which approach suits you. Follow current and popular music trends because the key to success to a business of this nature is all about who you know, and what you can bring to the table. It would be wise to establish relationships with Dj's and Club owners etc...

70) Independent Music Label- By marketing performers, new bands, everything from jazz to Hip Hop and rock and Roll; via the internet you could establish a business as an independent music label. With a wide variety of styles to suit everyone's taste the key to success will rest on your ability to secure the rights to musical acts, promote, sign, as well as market those

acts. Your start up cost may be high, but the profit potential would be even higher.

71) Modeling Agency- If you have great contacts and know how to capitalize on those contacts, starting a modeling agency just might be the business venture for you. Modeling agencies represent the people of appearance, size, shape, race; they are used to display and promote a service for their paying clients. This is a very competitive business and very profitable, once established the key is to start small and grow. It would also be wise to look for businesses that are doing commercials as well as print shoots, in order to build your agency.

72) Theater Production- Putting money behind a theater production as a producer, you'll need a director, a venue, and a technical team, once you have established this, you will need to know a little something about the theater this is where research come in, as well as theater management. You may find promoters, directors, and stagehands that will work for little or no financial compensation this is an opportunity for them to enhance their skills and build up their credit. Many other venues can also be secured for free providing there are benefits to the owner of the venue, such as product and refreshment sales. The key in producing income from producing a community play, retain as much of the ticket revenues as possible while seeking out ways to reduce and eliminate production cost. Selecting a well known musical would be a good way to start. Popular musical can and will generate the most ticket sales, higher prices and are familiar to perform and the audience would love this. This makes them easier to market.

73) Karaoke DJ Service- The requirement for starting a Karaoke DJ Service is quite basic.

- You'll need good karaoke equipment

- A great Music selection

- Reliable Transportation

- Good singing voice to market your service you would need to contact wedding planners, local night clubs, restaurants, as well as pubs and bars that would like to host a weekly karaoke Contest.

74) Standup Comic- Like acting there is very little money to be made unless you've proven yourself; it would be wise to perform at local comedy clubs where you can get stage time. Keep writing so that you will have at least 20 to 40 minutes of solid material. Working at a local club until you act is top notch. Get video or CD"s made to distribute to bookies of colleges, and nightclubs, establish something in your act that makes yours unique, something that makes people remember you, your look and character. You may also want to find a manager to represent you.

75) Entertainment Publicist- As an entertainment publicist you would be responsible for spreading the word in order to sell tickets for entertainment such as performers, film, and theater productions, getting your clients as much publicity as possible.

Your income, revenue would be generated by charging your clients a monthly fee in order to carry out your service. You would write blurbs, articles, mention them on television, radio and the internet, as well as newspapers and magazines. The key to success is being well connected in the media circles. IN the course of publicizing talent, film and books etc... You would be responsible for writing press releases, handling interviews request, as well as setting up press conferences, and other such events. If you are outgoing a sociable, organized, and love networking it's easy to start a business venture of this caliber from home, just start by building up your media contact list.

76) Location Scout- Location scouts find locations for film producers, television programs, and commercials by advertising agency and film studios to start out you'll need to have a strong contact base such as, producers, directors, and advertising agencies representatives who know they can contact you to get what they need. You'll also need a camera to take pictures of the numerous possible locations from alleyways, to ocean fronts, and mystical waterfalls, descriptive photographs or videos to present to your client and potential clients will be necessary. You'll be able to explain to the clients the best possible time of day would be proper for specific shoots, as well as having locations information available. Surrounding areas such as where the film crew can eat, where to park their cars, and what hotels they can stay in etc... location scouts are also responsible for how much the film company or advertising agency will pay for the location you present to them. You'll earn your income by being hired to scout and find locations.

77) Production Company- If you have experience in how to write, direct or shoot and edit a film or television programs and commercials you could work from your garage based studio or from home to start your business venture as a production studio for $50k to $75 k you could launch the business and attract clients for corporate video shoots land local commercial work, or short well based projects. The first year of production your might have to reinvest your income into the company to continually upgrade your equipment and seek studio space and build your business.

78) Check Cashing Service- A business of this caliber is very good to start. Payday loans and check cashing services to cash checks usually will charge their customers 35 of the total as a service charge fee. If you start your business venture with $1,000 dollars and cash checks for that amount everyday at the end of the year your income investment should bring in more than $1,095. In check cashing service fees 1,100% on your investment. Imagine 10, 20 30 times that amount on a yearly basis, an even higher rate can be earned on short term payday loans.

 79) Leasing Agent- A special license is not required to match clients with leading institutions that specialize in providing financial solutions on a lease basis to purchase ranging from automobiles to computer equipment for business use. Operating this service are very easy, simply secure clients wishing to lease a product and complete and submit the lease document to two or three leasing companies or financial institutions, the lender would reply with the best lease rate and terms for your client. Revenues earned for your service will be by charging the financial institution a commission based on the value of the total lease amount. Income profits potential range from $40,000 to $100,000 per year.

80) Business for Sale Brokers- It's common for a business broker to earn $250,000 or more per year after expenses provided they have the right skills. Your job would be to specialize in the listing and sale of businesses and commercial investment property. Finding and selling businesses in good locations and with the potential to be profitable for their new owners. All it takes is marketing can be by way of the internet, trade specifics, and publications and a wide list of network contacts within the industry.

81) Tax Prep Specialist- If you have accountant skills and background this might be the business venture for you, if not you can obtain your training through certified courses, this will give you the tools you need to start your own tax prep service. The more skills you have in a business of this caliber the more earning potential you will have even though this is a seasonal service. You can still earn an income year round by providing your clients with a bookkeeping service. Once you have established your tax prep service word of mouth advertising, and repeat business will support the service. To draw in clients consider offering them a 2 for one special during your first year of operation.

82) Licensing Specialist- As a licensing specialist, you can seek out opportunities to secure the exclusive rights to use a popular name brand product, service and operating system or formula, and sell sub license, to qualified business owners wishing to utilize the license in a business venture product or service. If you want to sell licenses, clothing to a clothing company to use the name or image and logo on their clothing ad charge them a

onetime fee plus going royalties based o the success of the clothing line. You can sell a license to a corporation that wants to establish a chain of restaurants using the name and logo and image, there are literally thousands of ways to profit as a licensing specialist. Start by learning as much as you possibly can about licensing and applicable laws.

83) Used ATM Sales- Sales of second hand ATM's while a nice lucrative income can be earned by purchasing and re-selling ATM's machines. The profit would be earned by placing the ATM machine in a busy location where it can generate revenue. The potential to earn over $250,000 per year is attained for the determined entrepreneurs who initiates this very basic business concept and place the ATM machines in the right location; location is the key to success.

84) Bookkeeping Service- if you possess bookkeeping and accounting skills, you could earn a substantial income by running a bookkeeping service. Most clients don't have the time or the ability to manage their books; this is where you come in, since the age of technology has advanced over the years. There are many small business bookkeeping and accounting software available. That will make your job a lot easier, and will also provide you with the tools to service many clients at once. Book keepers charge their clients a monthly fee to record and update their financial records on a regular basis this range from $25 to $30 bucks an hour.

85) Collection Agency-if you would like to start a business venture as a collections agent. You could operate from a home based office; your general focus would be to collect financial debts typically owned by a company or a business in a non harassing manner, plus utilize the telephone and official sounding letter as your main debt collecting tools. Securing your client base for this business is extremely easy, consisting you will not be compensated unless you successfully collect debt owed to that company. Your rates for your services are based on a percentage of the amount of money that is collected the longer the debt has not been paid, the higher the fee charged will be for collecting the debt. Typically 25% fee would be charged for successfully collecting debts beyond the point fees could increase to as much as 50% for the total debt collected.

86) Image Consultant- A image consultant keeps their corporate executives and business owners up with current fashion trends and social trends to maximize a favorable public image. Your business would be to assist clients in selecting the best social events to attend. They also help them keep up with current social and political issues. They also coach their clients on situations & conversations to avoid that could potential ruin their careers and their reputation. The potential income range from $30 to $50 bucks an hour or more depending on the client

87) Franchise Specialist- In order to build a successful business as a franchise specialist, you would need to form a joint venture with a lawyer or attorney who specializes in this field of

business, business law is crucial. Your business would consist of looking for small, independently owned businesses that are ideal candidates to be expanded nationally. This would be a more common way of operating this business; you would look for businesses that also have already gone through lengthy and costly franchising legal requirements process, and are now ready to begin marketing their franchises to qualified owners or operators. The goal is for you the franchise specialist to market the franchise, retaining a large portion of the franchise fee in exchange for providing the service and in some cases even retain some of the company's stock. This is a very lucrative business.

88) Sale Training Service- By training other sales professionals to also become top notch sales professionals, the training can be taught at the client's site or in a home based classroom. Te course curriculum can be developed by amassing your sales experience, techniques, and trade secrets, and methodology, into a study guide utilized and practiced by students. Gaining clients for the classes can be easy as creating and marketing packages. The promotional package should describe the sales training program. Highlight your own personal sales achievements, and explain the benefits and value that this package have, focus on the specialized coaching and the effects that this program could have as far as turning order takers, into sales makers. The marketing presentation can be presented to business owners and corporations that rely on a direct sales team to drive business revenues and profits

89) Independent Sales Consultants- Freelance sales consultants represent companies selling products and services ranging from manufacturing goods to home improvement services because freelance consultants generally supply all the tool of the trade, such as transportation, communication requirement, computer equipment that may be required to acquire customers and conduct business. With freelance consultant clients have little if anything to lose?

Remuneration of products or services sold always by the way of commission, which range from 25% of the total sales

90) Speaker Bureau- To organize and run a business as a speaker bureau you would have the task of gathering professional business men and women and arrange for them to do a public speaking event. By setting up speaking engagements for public speakers, you would have to decide which public speaker would be great for which speaking engagement. The best way to market such a service would be business brochures, fliers, and via the internet, by networking with conferences, colleges, and business and corporations. You can also promote and sell videos about speaking ad books on the topics.

91) Grand Opening Consultant- There are new businesses opening up all over America, what better way to cater to the small business person then to create an opportunity to start a business that specialize in catering to clients with various grand service packages.

- A Press Release Service

• A Red Carpet Service

• A Ribbon Cutting Ceremony Service Marketing this grand opening service, explaining your various business proposals should be easy, just consider initiating a direct mail campaign, the campaign would target new businesses that have recently opened or will be opening, simply contact your local business licensing center and get a list of all new businesses to solicit your packages to.

Contract Negotiation Service- Are you a good negotiator? If so, your negotiations skill could get you paid and would be a great asset in your new business venture. If business ethic just happens to be one of your strong points and you have great communication skills, as well as great closing skills, then a contract negotiation service is the business for you, by creating a market package explaining the service you offer, don't forget to mention past deals you may have negotiated. This would definitely be a plus in drawing in potential customers. Once your marketing package has been completed, you're ready to set up appointments with potential customers, and companies and business owners that need your service.

92) Contract Negotiation Service- Are you a good negotiator? If so, your negotiations skill could get you paid and would be a great asset in your new business venture. If business ethic just happens to be one of your strong points and you have great communication skills, as well as great closing skills, then a contract negotiation service is the business for you, by creating a market package explaining the service you offer, don't forget to mention past deals you may have negotiated. This would definitely be a plus in drawing in potential customers. Once

your marketing package has been completed, you're ready to set up appointments with potential customers, and companies and business owners that need your service.

93) Office Protocol Consultant- Are you good at settling disputes? If so what better reason to start a business getting paid for your expertise in settling matter between employees and management, your business would focus on situations such as racism, sexual harassment, abusive behavior, acting as an office protocol consultant you would advise clients based on all the above subjects and more…. Creating a program for employees and management to live by while in the work place, on how to avoid and react to certain situations. This is a great opportunity and has lots of potential clients and corporations who would rush to retain your services. It crucial to make sure you are educated on all the latest employment laws.

94) Marketing Consultant- Marketing is the number one factor in starting any business. This makes your business as a marketing consulting high in demand; marketing consultants generally specialize in one particular element, while experience consultants tackle a full range of marketing aspects for paying clients. There are a number of ways you can attract clients to your marketing consultant business, by networking, direct mail advertising, or you could set up meetings with potential clients to propose your marketing consultant service. If you are experienced in marketing using the internet is sure to specify your extra talents to your clients and capitalize on your abilities. Marketing consultants earn up to $100.00 an hour and up.

95) Debt and Bankruptcy Counselor- This is a rapidly growing business that you should tap into. Unfortunately, there are hundreds of thousands of consumers that file for bankruptcy

every day. In order to start a business of this nature you would need to know bankruptcy law, this is where research comes in, it wise to do your research about debt management also. If you have a background in banking or personal finance this would definitely be a plus for you. Your job would be to help your clients settle their debt, cut spending, in order to avoid filing for bankruptcy, if your clients have no other choice then to file you would guide them through the process. Your income would range from $50 an hour and up.

96) Used Restaurant Equipment- Starting a business venture that sells used restaurant equipment like fryers, and coffee machines, grills, refrigerators, stoves, plus deli equipment. A business such as this could start off working from a home base, sand once your business starts to grow you can move to a much larger facility. If you desire you could specialize in one kind of restaurant equipment. You r first step in entering the used restaurant equipment business would be to do the necessary research, and your equipment what is the going rate? For the equipment, you will also need a truck or access to a rental truck, and a storage unit to store your equipment once you start accumulating it. Once you've done your necessary homework the potential to earn large profits are definitely in the cards.

97) Prepackaged Energy Foods- If energy food is one of your business venture ideas, there is a large market for prepackaged energy foods and foods like mixed nuts, dried fruits, and raisins, and you can also produce your own line of energy drinks and full meals. You could also sell this product via the internet or websites or by listing your products for sale on other health food related websites.

98) Popcorn Cart- If you always dreamt of selling popcorn, this may be the terrific opportunity for you as a part time or full time business there are excellent profit in popcorn by pacing your popcorn cart in a high traffic area which includes the flea market, sports events, carnivals, fairs, farmers markets, or you could sale popcorn at community gathers. A business of this nature requires a little more than a vendor's license. A popcorn cart could cost you as much as 15,000 by purchasing a second hand cat you could as little as $2,000 or maybe $5,000 depending on the size of the popcorn cart and the condition the cart is in, you could actually make living selling popcorn.

99) Sandwich Delivery Route- A sandwich delivery route business could generate a profit of $1,000 a week easy, plus to start this business venture a delivery route is very inexpensive. You would get your clientele from office buildings, industrial workers, and surrounding cities and communities. The secret to success is the sheer volume of people working in these busy areas. Establishing a working relationship with catering services, delis, and restaurants that can supply you with sandwiches, salad etc... on a wholesale basis. While building up your customer base first and foremost, you would have to come up with a menu listing, all sandwiches and salads, and miscellaneous items. Your job would be to hire a crew or work alone distributing all the menu's to office buildings and facilitates, your potential customers would place their orders with you over the phone, or via email and course all deliveries would be free. You could make a hefty profit and more.

100) Farmer's Market- Why not start a farmer's market in your community this is a great business venture, everybody loves fresh veggies and fruit. By securing leases premises the vender's booth can be rented to local farmers. Specialty food manufacturers and craft vendor's could rent booths from you, the going rate for a booth these days on a farmer's market are $75 to $125 dollars a day, prior to operating expenses, the key to success in this type of business venture is to ensure. The vendor's have high quality products and the necessary licenses and permit to make your business idea a go, pass out fliers and promote your business around the community until area residence become familiar with it.

101) Coffee Service- Did you know that coffee could make you rich? Literally there are billions of cups of coffee sold every day in the U.S.A. alone. The profit potential is through the roof, a coffee service generally supplies companies with the coffee making equipment in exchange, the company would purchase coffee and coffee filters from the coffee service. Only if you operate on a large scale basis and your product is high quality, especially for coffee drinkers are very particular.

102) Juice Bar- Everyone is a potential customer when it comes to fresh squeezed juice, and juice bars are a new business enterprise, once you establish a location where business and traffic would be continual like a tourist attraction, the beach, or the food court at the mall, or fitness clubs, and public market places, the potential for profit includes additional items such as sandwiches and salads, and healthy food selections, you can also boost up the profits by considering a free delivery service

of fresh squeezed juice in large qualities. A well equipped and ran a juice bar can earn profits up to $50,000 per year, and profits can go much higher by adding additional items, doing more research is a must in order to know what healthy people really want to eat and drink.

103) Organic Farming- Operating a farm that grows organic food will require lots of research. A lot of people in our society only eat organic products and the profit potential in the ever expanding market is great. Your investment to get started would be extremely large, however there is a demand for organically grown foods and the market continues to grow and expand. Health conscious consumers are continually concerned about maintaining a healthy lifestyle and a well balanced diet.

104) Pizza By the Slice- For a small investment you could open a small pizzeria that offers customers a lot of advantages. For lower monthly overhead, and shorter operating hours, a takeout restaurant includes the food court in the local mall, store fronts in local business districts and a kiosk, supplying pizza on a wholesale basis to your customers by providing a free lunch time delivery service, serving up pizza slices in office districts can also boost up your business and sales.

105) Community Restaurant Guide- Why not start a business that creates monthly community restaurant guides? A guide of this nature would inform the community about restaurant specials and coupon saving as well as information about events

taking place in the community. The restaurant guide can be distributed throughout the community for free; you would earn your income by charging a fee to businesses featured in the community restaurant guide. Extra income can also be earned by charging restaurant and business owners with menu printing options, as well as paper place mat advertising and printing options.

106) Packaged Herb and Spices- A business venture of this stature can be created in a home base on a part-time or full time basis. By purchasing herbs and spices from a wholesaler or manufacture in bulk and repackage them into smaller quantity and sell the product through retail store via (POP) point of purchase, putting a display together is quite easy to do, just make sure whatever package design you create is unique. You also need to make sure that your (POP) display is visible in highly visible areas in whatever retail store you decide to display your herbs and spices. Your display would have to be placed on consignment with retailers, until the product proves to be a seller. Once your product proves to make the cut, the account can easily be converted to a typical wholesale supplier account. Consider supplying and stocking the display with cookbooks, and recipe guides as well this will increase your business revenues and profits.

107) Wedding Cake Sales- To have the talent to design and create wedding cakes is truly an art. This business opportunity could be a part time or full time opportunity. Many specialties designed wedding cakes can retail anywhere from $500 and up. To break into a business venture like this you would definitely

have to build up a working relationship with wedding planners and event planners & caters alike. Even if you might have to split the profits it would be well worth it for the extra business that will come your way, this is the fastest possible way to establish the business. Important fact: Be sure to check all local requirements in terms of operating this type of business, health board permits may be required. If you can't run this type of business from your homes, maybe you could rent a commercial kitchen on a part time basis during non business hours. Operating a wedding cake business can easily generate an income of $300 or more each week. You will also discover that if the cakes you make are unique enough, you will benefit from word of mouth advertising. Especially is you spread the word around in local wedding circles such as with wedding planners, event planners, florist, and photographers.

108) Roadside Vegetable Stand- A business like this is a seasonal one, the season being June to September. The startup cost are minimal, the demand for fresh vegetable are high which can mean the profit potential for a business venture of this nature would be high. Just remember location is the key to your success, excellent locations include near gas stations where traffic is always high, parking lots, industrial parks, and near main highways, or in and out of the busy tourist areas. You would have to secure all necessary business permits & licensing, and don't forget to create large colorful signs to attract potential customers.

109) Submarine Sandwich Shop- There are many great opportunities by opening this type of business venture. A business like this does not require a lot of experience or skill, just know how to make a great sandwich and you're in. Like all great business opportunities the key to success is finding the best location. You must cater top of the line customer service, and serve the best food for reasonable prices. The name of submarine sandwiches is also called hoagies, blimpies, grinders, subs; wedge and heroes, another way to expand your earning potential would be to add salads to your menu selection. There are two major restaurants that franchise such sandwiches, in order to gain a competitive edge it would be up to you to come up with a product that they don't serve on their menu selection, whether that may be wine, beer, desserts, etc….. Or something unique that sets your submarine sandwich shop apart from all the rest.

110) Gourmet French Fry Stand- If your dream is to sell French fries, since French fries are one of the most popular fast foods sold in America. You would need to find a very busy location to set up shop, such as the food court in the mall, beaches, the town square, or city parks, fairs, and carnivals are also good locations, or outside of busy office buildings. Of you want this business opportunity to work it would be quite impressive to add choice toppings, such as chili, cheese, chili salsa, gravy, or just any other topping you feel your customers would love. Your fries should always be freshly cut on site, in order to be considered the best. Consider purchasing used restaurant

equipment such as potatoes clippers, fryers; this will keep your start cost at a minimum.

111) Hot Dog Cart- A hot dog cart can retail anywhere from $4,000 to $8,000 depending on the features. This is a great business opportunity, however if you find that obtaining a vendor's license is at all difficult, you could still operate your hot dog cart on private property & cater to various functions such as: at the flea market, auctions, sports events, fairs, carnivals, and event in the park or at the beach. A business opportunity like this can be run full time or part time providing you serve your hot dogs at a good location, a hot dog vendor can easily earn income anywhere from $4,000 per month and more.

112) Catering Service- A catering business is a business that is always in demand, one of the best aspect of this type of business is that it can be run on a full or part time basis as the demand increase. To secure clientele for your catering service you would have to build up a working relationship with event and wedding planners, you may also want to create a marketing package to present to corporations, businesses, schools, and universities because they all use caters all the time. Your website should have a variety of catering packages to present to potential and existing customers.

113) Cotton Candy- The equipment needed to make cotton candy would cost you as much as $2,000. Starting a part time business making cotton candy requires a good location such as

fairs, carnivals, beaches, parks, and community gatherings, flea markets, kiosk, and birthday parties for hire. A cotton candy trailer or kiosk can operate on weekends only and you can still generate an income of $1,000 per day.

115) Fresh Pasta Making- You could start a business making fresh pasta, by proposing a joint venture with any restaurant you want just as long as that business serves fresh pasta. You make the pasta at their location, and they use the pasta for meal preparation for the business. As well as sell fresh pasta to their customers. A business like this can be established and operated in a food market or a farmers market by renting a booth, or a storefront, or kiosk. You could also generate extra income by selling freshly made sauce and seasonings.

116) Candy Store- To start a business selling candy one must have the right location. A candy store, a candy stand, or a kiosk in a very busy area would boost your profits extensively. Customers who want to buy candy for sick relatives in the hospital, or friends, at holiday time or business owners wanting to rewards existing customers or employees. There are so many business possibilities for your candy shop.

117) Buffet Only "All You Can Eat" Restaurant- Open at 11a.m. until 9p.m. all you can eat buffet restaurant have become an American favorite of the crowd on a budget, especially for the large family, or lunch time business crowd. There is one major advantage for the operator of this type of restaurant short work

days, only because you would generally cater to the lunch and dinner crowds. All and all buffet style restaurants can be very profitable just as long as you serve what the hungry crowds love to eat. Wholesale food items can be purchased for lower prices based on volume buying.

118) Exhaust & Hood Cleaning- Because of required health board regulations to prevent bacteria and grease fires, exhaust and hood cleaning business creates an opportunity for a business venture for you. Because the cleaning material and equipment can be so costly, there is specialized equipment available or you could also resort to, "Good ole fashion cleaning" income potential for a business of this nature varies depending on the size, style, and access, income earnings should be established at an hourly rate from $30 to $50 per hour for your cleaning expertise.

119) Specialty Sauces- Do you own any family secret recipes that you feel would be a hit on store shelves with consumers? Barbeque sauce recipes, salsa recipes, salad dressings, if so, you should consider sharing those recipes with the public by starting your own business that specializes in creating and marketing specialty sauces, and sell them in bulk to restaurants or package in small quantity and sell them in grocery stores, and specialty food retailers or on a wholesale basis First in foremost, your sauce must taste good, and your packaging must be unique in order to gain potential clientele's interest. The price must be in line with the competitor's price, and you also would need to promote heavily to get store shelve space. Be sure to enlist the

services of a product demonstration service to give away free samples of the product or do in store demo's yourself.

120) Soup and Salad Restaurant- Soup and salad restaurants are very popular with lunch crowds, and Sunday after church crowds, the income potential could virtually put you on the road to financial freedom. If you would like to open this type of establishment that caters to the business district, or office buildings with your community for the massive lunch crowds, or the restaurant could be located in the food court at the mall, or near an office district so that you could provide the hungry crowds with a quick meal or lunch time soup, salad and sandwiches also throw in free delivery service. Orders would be placed by email, telephone, or via fax. The income potential for such an establishment would be through the roof, if you serve good food, and have reasonable prices and provide top of the line service.

121) Employee Cafeteria- Everywhere you go like factories, schools, institutions, and corporations there's a cafeteria. These establishments are all owned by outside forces such as contractors who operate under a lease. This might be the business for you if you are seeking to start a low investment opportunity. If you would like to secure a lease for this type of business venture generally this would be obtain by successfully tendering the service, typically tenders for cafeteria services are put up for bidding every couple of years. It would be wise to do

the research more specifically look into the particular cafeteria you would like to operate before the contract runs out.

122) Doughnut Shop Wholesale Supplier- Doughnut shop the serve doughnuts, muffins, coffee, and tea and specialize in making doughnuts for wholesaling to grocery stores, restaurants, schools, and catering companies. Profit potential can range from $40,000 per year and up. Even though this business can be very competitive, be sure to do the research and planning before prior to stabling this as your potential business venture.

123) Ice Cream Stand- Everyone loves ice cream, it's just a proven fact. If you find a location you feel is in need of an ice cream stand. This may be the business venture for you. A stand like this could generate profits in excess of $50,000 and a shop would generate even more than an ice cream stand. You could even specialize in ice cream cakes, there are so many benefits if you decide mobile ice cream stands soot your taste, and you could take your mobile ice cream stand almost anywhere and become an instant hit with the kids.

124) Pr-packaged Vegetarian Foods- Pr-packaged vegetarian foods are not the easiest to find in your local grocery at least not in a large variety of entrees, Perhaps you could start a business that specializes in per-packaged vegetarian foods, your meal will be sold in grocery stores, and specialty food retailers. A business venture like this will require lots of research and

planning once that has been established, there is an upside to your profit potential and a long term business.

125) Vegetarian Restaurant- To open a vegetarian restaurant it would be best to conduct a consumer survey to establish an indication of the demand in your area. If you do decide to open your restaurant it is especially important to serve meatless meals as we as vegetarian cookbooks and guides this could be a good way to increase business revenues and profits, establish delivery service for homes, offices, this could also be a way to boost your profits.

126) Chuck Wagon- A chuck wagon is actually a delivery step van or enclosed trailers which have been converted into a food concession on wheels. You can find mobile restaurant businesses virtually everywhere. By equipping your mobile food concession on wheels with restaurant equipment such as fryer's, a microwave, grills etc… typically chuck wagons menu' include food such as French fries, hamburgers, hot dogs, etc… one of the best features about running a chuck wagon is you can make your own flexible hours. A good location is always the key to success. Location include: outside of an industry, factories, auction houses, sports events, fairs, carnivals, and the list go on. Another good fact is that in order for you to serve food to the public you would need the required permits and health board certificates to operate in public places. Consider your chuck wagon meets health codes, the permit should be easy to get. Profits range from $1,000 a day and up for a business like this located in the right location.

127) Catering Truck- A catering truck can be purchased for around $10,000 not only are the hours of operation, flexible, the morning from 6 a.m. til 3 p.m. you'll need food product to stock your catering truck, these can be purchased directly from restaurants, catering services, food wholesalers, catering truck routes include construction sites, factories, parks, beaches and sports events.

128) Take Out Chicken Wings - To start a takeout chicken wing restaurant business venture it's easy. Experience isn't easy to open a chicken wing joint. Location to set up would be the food court at the local malls, or a storefront, the business can also be established in a mobile enclosed trailer, or a van that has been converted into a mobile restaurant Just as long as you have met all health code regulations. You could also add a free delivery service for your customers, earning potential for this kind establishment is high.

129) Dessert and Pastries Shop- this type of dessert shop is very easy to run, a small sit down establishment that offers a variety of menu options such as cakes, pies, cookies, tarts, ice cream and a variety of other desserts that simply satisfies your customers sweet tooth. The best area to open a business of this nature would be a place where that is a high traffic area, such as malls, financial districts, near factories, etc…. Additionally, many items on the menu can be packaged and sold under the business name, and sold on a wholesale basis to establishments such as grocery stores, specialty food retailers if your desserts are good and yummy enough word of mouth will spread fast

concerning your establishment just as long as it's in a good location.

130) Cookie Sales-It's easy to mass produce, gourmet cookies, all you have to do is simply rent a commercial location and master the cookie making process. Design a package for your cookies and your ready to rake in the dough. Specialty gourmet cookies can be sold to retailers on a wholesale basis, or directly to the public & to gourmet shops, and restaurants or in a kiosk at the local mall, at movie theaters, and local sporting events, as a concession business. And if you ad low fat of diabetic cookies to your menu that are good and tasty you could tap into a whole other market.

131) Bakery- bakery's can operate on a wholesale or retail basis, and if you are interested in starting this kind of establishment from a store front location Selling baked good directly to customers or as a wholesale business selling baked goods. Creativity will help you stand out from the competition. Prepare to have a baker; your profit potentials are good for a bakery especially in your business is located in a good location. Whether you are selling football shaped cakes, dinosaur cakes, and kid's birthday cakes, special occasion and holiday cakes & pies, or exotic baked goods or novelty cakes the better the design the more customers you will attract.

132) Peanut and Nut Sells- You can start a money making venture by buying peanuts in bulk, and selling them packaged to

retailers on a wholesale basis. The nuts can be sold on consignment; don't overlook the possibility of selling the nuts from a vending machine provided the machines are installed in a good location. Locations such as malls, pubs, sport bars, pool halls, bars etc…. you could even have a cart selling the various nuts all these possibilities can bring a good profit.

133) Frozen Yogurt Shop- A frozen yogurt shop can be established at the beach, or a busy tourist area for full time income. The business can easily be operated on a seasonal basis only. Make sure your menu appeals to a wide variety of customers and potential customers.

134) Herb Gardening- in order to start a business of this nature learn as much as you can about herb gardening. A small herb garden in your yard can easily be converted into a cash producing business, dill, parsley, rosemary, cloves etc…. are just a few of the list of herbs that customers love and use every day. Plan the garden, grow your herbs, and design the herb package you want to use to promote your product, establish an account with merchants to sell your product. The rewards are a few extra thousand bucks each year.

135) Restaurant Washroom Cleaning Service- Restaurant owners and managers will need your washroom sanitation service. Your job would be to convince them to need you. To establish a relationship with these restaurants owners just offer your services the first time around for free. Like they say first

impression are lasting impressions, income potential for a business venture like this are from $15 to $25 bucks an hour.

136) Grocery Delivery Service- a grocery delivery service delivers customers' orders for a few bucks; the grocery store would bill their customers, market the delivery service, and manage the deliveries. Your job would be to simply deliver the groceries. Or you could establish a buying account with a grocery wholesaler & resell those groceries to your clients for a profit. , you will have to create a catalog of the grocery items you plan on keeping in stock. Grocery delivery services are very profitable businesses, as the convenience of home delivery makes getting customers very easy. By starting a website you could make this a very tech venture, if you could get the groceries to the customers quickly, this would be your key to success.

137) Seafood Sales- Seafood sales and home deliveries, fresh high quality seafood available such as fish, lobster, ousters can be purchased on a wholesale basis, and re-sold for a profit to consumers. You'll need to purchase or lease a delivery truck with a refrigerator or a freezer unit. Make sure you are able to purchase your seafood from wholesalers who have the freshest possible seafood. This business has great income, revenue with the delivery service you can use this as a powerful marketing tool. Profits earned are over $30,000 a year.

138) Personal Chef Service- to operate a personal chef service or take your love for cooking to the road a personal chef for hire Basically wherever there is a kitchen on site that you could use to advertise your service. People having events such as birthday parties, anniversary parties, special events, house parties, will want to hire you, all you'll need to bring is your personal chef skills in any one of the above gatherings. Personal chefs typically earn $50 buck and up per hour. If you're well known for your culinary skills you could even earn more.

139) Produce Shop- A produce shop must be located in a thriving populated area. And if you want to make a produce shop your business venture, where there is lots of foot traffic you could make your produce shop more appealing. Just by adding a juice bar, extra sit down space, so your potential customer and existing customers could sit down. A good method of increasing your customer base and income potential would be to establish an account with restaurants catering to companies. Sky would be the limit for this business venture.

140) Deli- If you are interested in opening a deli, you would have to supply your customers with various meats, cheeses, and other exotic gourmet foods, but you could also supply your customers with lunchtime delivery service. A couple of seats and tables for the customers to sit down at lunch time, and take out service, and catering service would also add an additional income revenue to your deli. Include cold meat and cheese trays, party platters for corporate parties, the key to success is location, such as office districts, strip malls, and just as long as

you provide great customer service, and a variety of quality products.

141) Chef Wait Staff- Wherever there is catered events there is a need for a wait staff, and busboys. This opens up the kitchen door for you to start up a business whereby you is the one source for caterers. When people have private parties that are in need of your services, you could your business of by running ad's this will likely mean reaching out to college students, actors, dancers, and performers of all types would need work. The larger the area you cover, the more money you'll make, do a website which you can provide party planners, and event planners with the wait staff they need.

142) Water Ices- ices are very easy to sell, especially in the summertime, kids love them. You could opt for a cart in a full fledged location. If you want to sell watermelon, banana, lemon, cherry, mango, chocolate, or a 100 more flavors. You can start a business like this with a couple of thousand dollars, all it takes is having the best possible location, and the water ices will sell themselves.

143) Sushi Bar- there a lot of cash in a sushi bar, a refrigerator unit, a sushi prep table, a sushi display case, plus table chairs, and a sushi chef with is mandatory. Location will be your prime concern and I this case a high traffic area will be the place to open such an establishment. Location such as a mall, a strip mall

area where there are lots of potential customers who love to eat sushi.

144) Exotic bakery- from specialty designed cakes, erotic baked goods for bachelor parties, and bachelor parties, ad an interesting array of chocolates to non exotic specialty cakes. This will generate plenty of dough; you could market your store too soon to be brides and grooms as well as couples celebrating their anniversary.

145) Gourmet Shop- A small retail space in a upscale location what carries a variety of cheeses, smoked salmon, caviar, truffles, and hard to find delicacies can provide you with a regular clientele base that enjoy gourmet treats. Malls, kiosk, a satellite locations or even a wine shop will carry your gourmet products. Just learn your product well, provide good customer service, set up access for placing orders on your website.

146) Furniture Delivery and Assembly- The profit you could make turning abandoned furniture into cash. The best aspect of this business is that you don't even know how to repair, or refurbish the appliances yourself. The market for refurbished appliances is absolutely gigantic. Some appliance sells for as much as $5,000 to interior decorators, homeowners, seeking the designer touch. Refurbished antique appliances can be sold directly to your customers, and designer professionals via a display booth, at home or garden shows, advertisement in

home improvement and antique show publications or via the internet and website auctions such as eBay.

147) Junk Furniture Creations- A business like this can generate a six figure income. Starting a business that manufacture and sell junk furniture is a very lucrative venture. The key to success if to create funky, couches, chairs are the most popular, starting this type of business have it pre requisites creative and artistic ability. A well equipped workshop& design and construction skill will set you art from other businesses, a profitable business awaits you.

148) Mattress Shop- Mattress and bedding products have a life span of five years, starting a business selling mattresses and bedding products you should consider adding institutional, hotel, hospitals, and nursing homes to your list. These kinds of sales can add a huge amount of revenue to overall yearly sales. Selling linen purchased in bulk wholesale can bring additional revenues.

149) Skin Care Products- Research will definitely be the starting point for this business venture. To keep the start up cost to a minimum, start with basic skin care products, and expand from there the best possibility for an advertising medium would be the internet, promotional flyers, news paper ads, and shopping parties. Bu the best advertising will be from word of mouth. If your clients are they will spread the word, before you know it you will be well on your way to financial freedom.

150) Day Spa- Starting a day spa is an excellent choice for a business venture, finding the best location would be the most important aspect of this enterprise and supplying your day spa clients with a variety of services such as manicures, seaweed wraps, aroma therapy, and massage options will make your day spa a guaranteed success. You should have no problem charging top dollar for your services, providing you offer specialized, personalize service to your clients. You can advertise your day spa through traditional advertising mediums, be sure to print and distribute 2 for 1 discount coupons for the initial grand opening. You may have to sacrifice some revenue, but discount coupons are a great way to gain new prospective clients. The income and profit potential will depend on a number of factors, such as service offered, customer volume, and your business location.

151) Organic Hair Care Products- You could operate a hair care business from home, one opt would be to manufacture, create, and sell natural hair care products such as shampoos, conditioners, and made 100% natural organic ingredients. There will be research that will have to be done in terms of developing the products, the library, and the internet, should be quite helpful. Make sure the health requirements and keep the word "hypoallergenic" in mind. The other option is to buy products from various distributors and sell them to your customers through a website, local beauty salon, and even direct mail.

152) Home Care Service- A business of this nature would be well suited for someone with training and background in the health care industry, for someone who doesn't have the background there are training programs available. There are two kinds of home care providers and the training required for each one is different. The first type of home care service is one that focuses on assisting people with everyday task, such as cooking, cleaning, run errands, and personal hygiene. The second is a service that includes medication administration and in some cases therapy. This will mean advance training and some States may require a certificate. The income potential range from $20 per hour to as much as $50 per hour depending on the service provided and skill level required.

153) Hair Salon- There are many approaches for one who wants to start a business venture in the hair salon business. The first approach would be operating from a fixed location, and the second would be to go mobile. Consider the following aspects of the business.

Location- can include a home base, providing proper zoning is in place or can easily be secured. An indoor mall, a strip mall, even a lobby, retail area, or a retirement home, large office buildings, and complexes

Competition and Pricing- what does the competition charge for service? Can a profit be reasonably returned on your investment? What can you do to gain a competitive edge?

Quality of Service- Are you professionally trained barber or stylist, who provide excellent cuts, and have a rapport with customers, you can generate a lot of return business just make sure you have certified stylist and hair cutters on deck.

 Environment- A salon can benefit from the right ambience, know your demographics market and decorate accordingly. Once all the above things have fallen into place you will be very profitable and successful owning a salon.

154) Hair Removal Service- Starting a business venture doing hair removal is very profitable, proving you and your staff are trained and certified. The least expensive way to get the service started is to form a joint venture with an established business such as salons and day spas. A joint venture could reduce overhead cost and you'll also be able to capitalize off your partner's client base to jump start the business.

155) Perfume- To create, package, and distribute your own perfume line this business venture can make you quit rich. Developing the line will take a lot of research. Working with a chemist can be very useful for this type of business venture. Consider an all natural approach wherein the ingredients are concerned, because all natural products are the wave of the future. The perfume once developed can be sold to retailers on a wholesale basis, or directly to consumers via the internet, or you could establish a perfume kiosk in the mall, wherever there foot traffic, there are numerous advertising avenues you could take by advertising the perfume in a specialty publication you could generate a lot of mail order customer this way. Just make sure you secure the patent your scents.

156) Massage Oil- Development a massage oil line had great income potential. It would be wise to develop your oils from an all natural organic ingredient. Seek out joint ventures with established companies that can assist you in the development, marketing and distribution of your product. Joint venture may mean you would lose some of the control of the product and profits, but in the end they lost will be well worth it, considering the gain you will get from the sweet smell of success.

157) Health Taxi- Starting a health taxi service in your community may be a unique business venture. Purchase, lease, or rent suitable mode of transportation such as a passenger van. Set up accounts with local doctor's or dentist and health professionals in the community to provide their patients with a way to get to and from doctors appointments via health taxi service. The doctor would pay a flat fee that services taxied to the doctor's office, not only will the patient benefit from the free taxi service, but the doctor will also benefit by making sure that patients can get to them to receive proper medical care. Be sure to check out all the legal aspects of the business in terms of liability insurance as well as special driving permits.

158) Health Fair- Health care professionals and industry related healthcare companies could potentially become your clients. If you decide to start a business that promotes & host two day health fairs. A health fair is the same as a trade show or craft show. The major difference is that all of the vendor's or exhibitors' are in the health care industry. This unique related health care business has a chance of becoming very profitable, Charge admissions for attendees as well as exhibitor's fee for

booths. The key is finding a good location to hold the fair, spread the word in newspapers, magazines, and via the internet.

159) Medical Billing Service- Many billing practices are turned over to medical billing services. You can save medical facilities a great amount of time and effort, by handling the billing process and tracking down unpaid claims. If you can run an efficient office, and stay on top of outstanding bills, you could start this kind of medical billing service. It helps to have a background in the health care industry, this can also be launched as a home based business, Design a brochure explain your services and plans for billing, follow up and collect payment, and evaluate it to doctor's offices and medical group.

160) Fencing Installation- To start a fencing installation business, you must first start by determining the fencing material and style of fencing your services will be installing. There are various types of material used in fencing such as cedar, wood, pressure treated wood, store, brick, steel, or cast iron, recycled plastic, cedar rail, chain link, vinyl, and aluminum. There are also various methods that can be employed to promote and market a fence installation service to people such as contractors, subcontractors, and renovation companies, direct retail sales via advertising and installation only in home building and renovations centers.

161) Window Installation- People who possesses renovation and installation backgrounds will find this business start up to be interesting. Market yourself in conjunction with retail outlets that sells replacement windows, as well as through local ads in Penny Saver and by way of handouts at home expos and trade shows.

162) Ceramic Tile Sales and Installation- Ceramic tiles will always be a popular choice for flooring finish, due to their low maintenance, and high durability features. To become a successful installation professional in a business venture of this nature you will need experience and knowledge in the installation of ceramic tile flooring or have access to qualified tradesmen to do the actual flooring installation. Operating as a subcontractor service and renovation company would be the logical starting point.

163) Siding Installation- Siding sales and installation are almost as straight forward as a home improvement business selling the siding and installing the siding, pricing for siding products and installation is generally based on a per square basis. There are like any home improvement or renovation service, upgrades to the standard package that can make available to customers. Computer software can allow you to scan in a photo of the correct siding as it looks before you work, and then you can show what it will look like in an after photo to give the client an idea of what you can do.

164) Disposal Bin Service- to open a business of this nature, the home renovation and construction industry creates an enormous amount of waster each year, that has to be disposed of into landfills sites, or taken to recycling facilities for a renewal lease on life. There are a few different approaches to own and operate your own roll off or whiner truck that is used in the transportation and delivery and pickup of the disposed bins. The second options are to own only the disposal bins and sub contract. The delivery and pick up service to a trucking firm, the second option is less expensive in terms of startup cost. The third option may be most interesting it is to use tandem axle trailers which can be purchased second hand relatively inexpensive and can be towed behind anyone ton truck disposal service. With less money while controlling all aspects of the business and revenue, disposal rates are generally charted on a flat fee basis that is based on distance traveled. Make sure you have the necessary permits and licenses for this type of business all that you have authorized to unload at specific locations.

165) Carpet Installation- The main requirements for this type of business is to have the ability to properly install carpet or have access to qualified installers. The key to building up the business is showing your work which may mean doing a few jobs for free in exchange for taking photos of the work, show potential clients and or using the recipients of the free installation jobs you have done. Once you have demonstrated your work in a few locations you will get word of mouth referrals. Carpet installation professionals can make $25 per hour or more.

166) Dry Wall Installation- Dry wall trade requires lots of practice to master it, it's the fastest way to establish and expand a drywall business, to market the service directly to home owners and home builders and renovators. Marketing your service to home painters, and fire and flood restoration companies, as these companies can provide you with plenty of work, Companies like the subcontractor to an outside dry wall contract. Dry wall rates from $50 per hour plus the material and repairs are $1 to $1.25 per square foot for new finished drywall installation.

167) Deck Building- Installing, designing, and building sundeck for a business venture is a good way to earn a nice living. Many retail for as much as $15,000 and include the features such as build in planters, area for sunken in hot tubs, glass or cast iron hand rails, and custom manufactured wood furniture. The best way to get rolling in the sundeck, business includes subcontracting for establishing building renovation companies, designers and architects and also potential clients. You could also market your sundecks services directly to consumers via the internet, showroom or through trade shows displays. The total start up cost will vary greatly depending on the type of sundeck built and installed your investment will range from $15,000 to $20,000. The potential for sundecks sales and installation service can greatly vary. Potential profits range from $30,000 to $100,000 per year.

168) Closet Organizers- Closet organizers are very popular and relatively very easy to install. All it requires are a few basic hand tools, and reliable transportation. You can market your service

yourself from a home base and home renovators as well as to consumers through advertisements. Home expos, or on your website or even fairs, the profit potential from $40,000 per year is easy to attain.

169) Pet Doors- The best way to break into this business is to market the installation service yourself through pet stores, this could be a great way to market your new business venture. The pet stores in your community shall have no problem assisting you as they will be selling the doors, and retaining their retail markups. You could even manufacture, retail and install the pet doors for a maximum profits return. Do your research and contact retail chain pet stores, even though they may sale the pet doors, they may not install them. This is where your services come in. Product samples, advertising, and marketing budget, you could charge a rate of $25 to $40 per hour.

170) Garage Organizers- Starting a garage organizing service requires no experience or equipment, rather than basic tools, you could offer your services to start with family and friends. Garage organizers are typically various shelf configurations or storage bins; you could buy such items wholesale and provide them with free delivery and installation. Home improvement Tradeshows will be a valuable source. Such a display can cost you less than $1,000 to set up. You could maintain an hourly rate $25 to $35 and up.

171) Mirror Installation- Mirrors are required for just about all residential and commercial businesses washrooms. A mirror installation and sales business can be easy to operate from a home garage. All that is required is a truck with a basic glass rack, a few tools, and the ability to cut glass. The current rate of installation, bathroom mirrors is in the range of $5 to $7 per square foot. While the wholesale cost of the mirrors is only $2 per square foot, once you have established the business you can begin marketing the services to commercial and residential construction companies.

172) Hot Tub Installation- hot tubs make a good addition to any home. The focus of this new business opportunity is not aimed at hot tub sales but shot tub installation. In order for the hot tub to work properly and safely it must first be installed correctly, including the electrical hookup, and solid foundation base, potential customers, including hot tub retailers who require additional installation contractors and homeowners who are moving and require hot tub relocation. You could provide a hot tub cleaning service as well.

173) Sales Installation- A business that sells and installs safes can be a lucrative one. A safe comes in two forms, the first being the traditional floor model safe that can be cemented into place as a safety measure, and the second mounted safes which are concealed behind furniture or installed in unlikely places such as an attic and closets and behind the pictures. Installing safes doesn't require any special certificates; the person carrying out the installation should be branded for insurance purposes. Find out the necessary regulations in your areas, the

capital required to activate this business venture is in the range of $2,000 to $5,000. The profit potential for safe installers they usually charge a fee of $200 per hour to install a floor or wall safe.

174) Door Installation- newly installed door not only have better, but safety and insulation features. Those doors are also highly attractive and can improve the appearance of the home for a relatively small investment. Due to the fact that this is a competitive industry, you may want to specialize in one particular type of door or become an exclusive agent or representative for one door manufacture. Specializing in any industry will eventually generate results, in lower wholesale products cost and higher returns.

175) Bathroom and Kitchen Vents- this is a great opportunity for a home base business venture that can generate a lucrative income. Installation of ventilation systems generally requires a few hours of your time and materials that can be purchased at any local building center. Design sample doors hanger flyers, and distributed them throughout your community can promote your service. Total start up cost will be less than $1,000, and your income level will be at least $600 per week.

176) Roof Installation- The first step in setting this business into motion is to decide on what type of roofing and building you will concentrate your marketing efforts. Depending on the type of roof replacement service, you will be operating the

requirements may vary in terms of skills and skilled staff. Equipment regulations and operating locations make sure you look into all kinds of necessary licensing and certificates, liability insurance is another must

177) Glass Tinting Service- This is an affordable service to launch, but the best aspect of the business is the fact that it can be operated on a year round basis, regardless of the weather conditions right from a mobile installation vehicle. The market for glass tinting is endless terms of residential, commercial, and automotive applications, including cars, boats, house windows and skylights, retail store windows, and residential windows. If you build up a relationship with used car dealers, boat brokers, and commercial property manager's sky's the limit.

178) Custom Fire Place Mantels- Mostly new fire places have one thing in common, they require a mantel to suit the fireplace, building and installing custom fireplace mantels is a great business venture. This kind of business can easily be started for under $1,000 and be operated right from a truck or van. In terms of marketing the mantels there is an endless supply of potential customers can provide you with work.

179) Customer French Doors- Start your own business the manufacture, retail and install custom made French doors. This is an excellent way to be self employed ad generate very lucrative profits. There are very little competition in this business, especially in the higher end market, such as expensive

homes and professional offices. A great way to market the French doors and installation service would be to work, home builders who are prepared to offer your French doors to their clients as an upgrade finishing option. This business will allow you to be creative in your designs, which can assist you in building solid reputations on the client base.

180) Glass Block Installation- Glass block is back in vogue for two reasons, having glass block windows installed is a cost effective to beautify your home and add real designer flair. The second reason is installing glass block into your basement window's area is a great way to let the light shine in, and at the same time burglar proof your windows. Starting a service like this doesn't require a lot of terms of experience and expertise, almost all home improvement centers will now make up glass block windows on a custom order basis.

181) Wall Paper Service- Commercial wall paper application is on the rise, if you decide to specialize in commercial wall paper finish, as oppose to paint finish it last longer, it is easier to maintain, and calculated over a useful life span it half the cost of painting. This is very inexpensive business s venture that you can initiate and can earn a comfortable living.

182) Home Theater- Big screen flat panel televisions, surround sound, computer technology, and state of the art audio components are all helping to fuel the demand for the perfect family entertainment room. Starting a business that specializes

in the design and turning a basement into a home theater is fantastic business. This is a business that can generate hundreds of thousands of dollars.

183) Green Houses- There is various approaches that can be taken for starting a greenhouse installation business. Designing and selling and installing green houses, designing and selling u0 install green houses, selling and installing greenhouses for existing manufactures. You could choose to so all the above and help people in selecting the plants and selecting up their greenhouse while charging accordingly. Your profit potential will range from $20,000 per year part time and $50,000 full time.

184) Fire Place Installation- Considering a fireplace installation business, you can install and sell all of these types of home fireplaces, only if you are planning on starting a fireplace installation business. The best way to operate and market his kind of business is with the assistance is with a fully operated fireplace showroom. For a business like this the profit potential will greatly vary, for a fireplace installation and sells person should be experienced as a contractor or a constructor with the ability to be able to complete a job in a reasonable amount of time. There should be no problem maintaining your profit margin of 25 to 30 % on all retail sales.

185) Paint and Wallpaper Store- Starting a paint and wallpaper store is relatively a stable retail business venture, to boost sales

and profits beyond just selling paint and wallpaper, you could also provide customers with unique services such as after hours instruction classes, in various home decorating mediums, and other product and services such as equipment rentals for do it yourself painters, factoring in considerations such as competition, start up investment, operating cost, and profit potential.

186) Above Ground Pools- If you interested in starting a business venture installing above ground pools, the first step you will need to take is to locate a manufactured and negotiate an executive distribution & installment agreement. Once that has been established you can advertise, promote and market while utilizing all the above methods. You could also add the service of pool maintenance, pool dismantling, and re installation for your client's relocation. Additionally you could also offer accessories such as pool filters, covers, and slides.

187) Garage Door Sales and Installation- This would make a great business opportunity because garage doors and accessories are not hard to install. The manufacture of this type of product usually includes detailed step by step instructions that basically walk you through the installation procedure. The keys to success lies in securing a distribution or installation agreement with one or more manufactures, there are hundreds of companies that manufacture garage doors in every style, material, selection and price range. If you build up a business relationship with new home builders, renovator or general contractors, real estate brokers, and agents and property managers to secure your services, and supply your business

with subcontractors, you could also market to home owners. By securing an ad in the newspapers or magazines and home improvement publications, you will be well on your way to establishing your dream of becoming a garage sale and installation business owner.

188) Sun-room Installation- Having a sunroom is a very popular addition to a home, to start a business venture of this nature, there are two options, the first option would be to contact a manufacture who supplies pro- built sun room kits, if you develop a working relationship with a manufacture you can negotiate an executive dealer agreement, the second option would be to build custom sun rooms to meet your customers' needs. Check local building and code regulations before considering getting started in this business, you need only basic construction knowledge to break into the sun room installation business. If you don't want to build a sunroom on your own you can hire a subcontractor to do the installation for you, while you dedicate your time to sales, marketing, and management. You gross profit margin should maintain a 50% markup at all times on your products. There is a 33 % on sales and marketing cost.

189) Ceiling Fans- Ceiling fans can be sold at the flea market, home decorating shows, or from a kiosk in the mall, a business installing ceiling fans range from $25 per hour, the key to success of running a successful ceiling fan business is to have ceiling fans on hand, by offering a repair service. It's also wise to have liability insurance safety should be your primary concern.

190) Residential Landscaping- If you have a background in horticulture and landscaping, and are good at designing yards, you could start a business in landscaping for residential and commercial owned properties. Landscaping consists of building patios, stone walls, plants, and gardening, anything that has something to with beautifying a home or commercial property. Do massive research and learn as much as you can about landscaping and how to beautify a yard or commercial grounds. Take photographs on the work you do before and after the work is done, and market your landscaping service to home owners, real estate brokers, home shows, trade shows, it would also be wise to create a brochure and a customized website to attract business and new clientele.

191) Custom Closet- If you have a background in carpentry starting a business building custom closet could be the business for you. Start up cost would possibly be in the range of $90,000 and marketing cost would probably be in the range of $30,000, the key to success is to always give the client what they want, if you could design a custom closet, or a multi functional closet then the skies would be the limit for you. Not to mention word of mouth advertising would attract more clients.

192) Window Treatment- The window treatment business is a very lucrative one, vertical blinds, curtains, drapes and if you carry a variety of products you could market your business through ads, fliers, and word of mouth advertising, you could even put together a brochure or catalog with pictures describing your services.

193) Graffiti Removal Service- A graffiti removal service is a great business opportunity, only because this is an untapped market. There are two major pieces of equipment that you will need in order to remove graffiti

• The first piece of equipment you'll need is a sandblaster.

• The second a pressure washer. For a profitable business of this nature your profit margin will easily generate $6,000 per month. The best way to market your business would be to check out potential clients who are often victims of unsightly graffiti, check in on businesses, schools, libraries, churches, apartment complexes who are often time victims of vandalism.

194) Mobile Screen Repair- There is a lot of screens that need to be repaired or preplaced. To start up a screen repair business it only requires a couple of basic tools a milter saw, a screen roller, and various screen materials and screen replacement vast. The best way to find clients for this business would be to establish a working relationship with companies & businesses and homeowners who might want to retain your services. These companies can include management firms, government agencies, community associations, etc... An established mobile screen repair service can generate earnings potential of as much as $100,000 per year provided you can cover wide areas.

195) Driveway Sealing- Starting a business venture as a driveway sealing company the only thing you'll need is asphalt and driveway sealer and a bucket, you will find that all the necessary supplies and equipment for such a business are available at home improvement centers. The potential earnings

for a business venture of this nature would start off at about $20 per hour.

196) Roof Repair- In order to start a business as a roof repairer you will need to research the various types of roofs. Start advertising your business to a variety of business owners whether residential or commercial. Advertising your skills and business can be done in the newspapers, yellow pages, or a promotional flier. You could also subcontract your business services to clubs, home repair associations, to establish an alliance with community property managers and maintenance companies.

197) Handyman Service- There is always a demand for a good handyman. The main requirement you'll need is that you are a "Jack of All Trades" a handyman's billing rates range from $30 to $80 per hour plus materials and markups on the materials cost and tools. You can advertise your services to commercial and residential clients alike. Advertise through home improvement clubs, the yellow pages, and newspaper advertisements, plus fliers and business cards distribution, you will also need a good amount of liability insurance before considering getting started

198) Welding- Before even considering starting a business as a welder, you will need to have a welder's trade certificate. Once you've established that, you could set up your welding business either from a home base or you could have a mobile welding

business. There are two forms of billing rates; the first gives your clients a cost estimate of the hourly rate. The second gives your clients a cost estimate of the job. The current welding rate range from $45 to $65 per hour overall a well established welder service can easily generate yearly profits in excess of $70,000

199) Home Storage Solution- You can profit by starting a business that specializes in home storage solutions. A business like this does not require a lot of investment capital. You can charge an hourly rate to install home storage products, search the internet and directories for manufacturing, simply contact them and tell them you would like to be a sales agent or representative of their products in your city or community. A business of this nature can grow by word of mouth and referrals; if you are an expert in the field of installing these products this can increase your profits.

200) Zinc Strips and Moss Removal- Zinc strips and moss removal is a business that's easy to set in motion. A business venture of this nature involves removing moss accumulation that can cause build up and structure problems. The most fast and efficient way to market this business would be to design informational fliers explaining the service you offer. Describe the business to homeowners and businesses that have visible moss problems, potential income range from $20 to $30 per hour.

201) Mobile Paint Spraying- Mobile paint spraying service is a profitable business to start and manage. The best way to run this business is to transport the paint spraying equipment I a small truck or trailer and paint items outside. You services can be marketed to both homeowners and businesses. You can spray paint everything from concrete floors, trailers, appliances, fencing, metal roofing, signs etc... Profit potential would be between the ranges of $35 to $50 per hour plus the cost of equipment and paint.

202) Gutter Protection- A gutter protection business is a profitable business. The product quickly snaps into place over the top of 4 or 5 inch gutters. The gutter protection allows water to pass into the gutter, but not debris. Many homeowners are not aware that there's a product like this on the market. To promote the product you will need to design and distribute promotional information flyers which will highlight all the benefits of the product. This business can be started for less than $1,000, but the income potential is $50,000 or more per year.

203) Fire and Flood Restoration- To start a business as a fire and floor restorer service, you will be responsible for assisting homeowners in repairing the damage resulting from fire or flood. Your duties would be to carry out immediate or temporary measures to limit any further unfortunate circumstances to the home or business, duties such as boarding up the property, or removing water that have accumulated inside the building, other duties include repairing damaged floors and walls as we as the structure of the property. You will

need to have experience in construction if not you can hire a subcontractor to do the work for you, make sure you are insured. The pay rate for a job necessary to ratify the damage, a business of this nature can grow from word of mouth referrals.

204) Fence Repair- A fence repair business can be started for less than $1,000, design a fence repair estimate form, leaving a blank area for a description of the repairs to be completed. Once you have printed at least 100 fliers and estimate forms, simply drive around the community looking for fences that need repairing, leave a flyer and business card for homeowners. Aim to close 25 % of the fence estimate that you complete. Profit potential for a fence repair business is $25,000 a year and up.

205) Window and Door Repair Service- Wooden windows and doors require yearly maintenance; the reason to target these kinds of homes is because the owners of old houses have wooden sash doors and windows. The demand for this type of service will always be steady employment for you. The income potential range from $20 to $35 per hour, and does not forget liability insurance.

206) Hard Wood Floor Sanding- You could start a business venture sanding hardwood floors. You could rent floor sanding equipment until the business has built up its client list, and has become an established profitable business. Sanding is usually billed by per square foot basis, so, it would be wise to check out current rates. Market your new business to subcontractors,

local construction companies, and renovation companies; you should have no problem creating a yearly income in the range of $40,000 to $50,000 per year.

207) Home Numbers On Curb- You can start a business venture like this for less than $100, having a house number painted on the curb for two professional reasons with high reflection paint. In the event of a 911 emergency the personal can locate the house day or night. The only equipment you'll need is a number stencil and a paint brush, simply design a door hanger marketing brochure that details all the benefits of your low cost service, hang them on every door in the community, the more door hangers you hang the more business you'll attract. Make sure there is no community restriction as such painting on the curb. You may also approach tenant committees, and neighborhood associations, and property managers provided you approach 10 to 20 clients a day. Charge a service fee of $20 for your service. The business can easily generate earning of $50,000 per year for this part time job.

208) Bath Tub Re-glazing- Start a bathtub re-glazing service requires very little experience, and the equipment is available through paint supply stores. This service is best marketed through establishing a working relationship with industry related businesses, such as property maintenance companies, construction companies, who would utilize your service for their clients. You can also set up a demonstration booth at home and garden trade shows. Income potential will vary by factors such as material cost, operating overhead, and once your business

has been established you can easily generate an income in the range of $40 to $50 per hour.

209) Basement Remodeling- The main requirement for a business venture of this nature is to have construction knowledge and experience. The business can specialize in one type of basement remodeling in general. Once the business has an excellent client base the profit potential will be great. Take "before" and "After" photos of your work and make a brochure, and start up a website featuring the photos. A business venture like this will require liability insurance.

210) Patio Deck Repair- For a business venture like this you will need some carpentry skills and knowledge of deck finishes, paint, and a wood cleaning chemical. And a few thousand dollars to start up, this can also be started up as a home based business venture. You can market your services at home and garden shows, through fliers, and direct mailing campaigns, this step should help you build up your clientele to whom you'll offer a 3 year service contract, and make sure you're up on the latest waterproofing and UV protection when you start this business venture.

211) Power Washing Service- if you are considering a business venture as a power washer, there many benefits to such a business, such as low investment cost, consumer demand, no inventory, there are also hundreds of items that can be power washed such as mobile homes, driveways, recreational vehicles,

signs, headstones, cars, boats, decks and patios, once you have secured repeat customers through marketing your service to companies, and individuals. Potential repeat customers could include construction companies, retail businesses, residential and commercial businesses, boat dealers, start up cost can range from $6,000 to $15,000 the only fixed overhead includes, the telephone, liability insurance, and transportation. However an established power wash service income can range from $40,000 per year and up.

212) Rubbish Removal Service- There are many potential customers for this kind of business, especially people who are preparing to sale their home and hoarders. If you build up a working relationship with real estate companies, and sales people to recommend your rubbish removal service to their clients, all you'll need is a truck, van or trailers, garbage cans, and a couple of shovels and rakes. Before starting make sure other agencies do not have licenses to handle specific areas, and also look into zoning laws and other ordinance that dictate where you can dump the rubbish once it's removed.

213) Roof Tune Up Service- Roof tune ups are proactive maintenance measures an opposed to a reactive measures, such as repairing a leaky roof, the average cost is $5,000 to replace a roof, for repairs up to 1,000. A roof tune up service, simply carries out annual roof inspections and corrects any minor problems. Clients can range from residential to commercial buildings, if you can provide your clients with a one year warranty, the warranty will provide your clients with on a basis should a roof that has been tuned up start to leak within

the one year from the date of inspection. Creating a warranty for this type of business is a great marketing tool; it gives your clients a sense of security when securing your services. Charge your clients $125 for an annual roof tune up, if you secure at least two tune up jobs per day, you can generate a yearly income of $65,000. The operating cost for this business is minimal, and only around 5% of the service charged. Once established hire subcontractors to service the account on a profit hare basis.

214) Pool and Hot Tub Maintenance- A hot tub most be cleaned and maintained on a regular basis, a pool and hot tub service can be marketed in all traditional advertising mediums. Consider distributing fliers and coupons should throughout your local community, the fliers and coupons should feature free pool and hot tub water safety test for owners of these items. The safety test will simply be testing the water for toxins and recommend any corrective measures that should be taken to fix the problem. This business could be very profitable during certain months.

215) Fire Equipment Testing- Many communities have regulations that require residential and commercial fire safety equipment such as alarms, extinguishers, to be tested and inspected on a regular basis. Starting a business that conducts fire and fire safety inspections can also profit from selling fire safety products, and equipment to residential and commercial clients, as well as installing the products.

216) Home Construction Cleanup- A home construction cleanup service can generate profits in excess of $60,000 per year, but it can also be started for an investment of less than $1,000. A construction clean up service should be inclusive meaning that the windows are cleaned, and the entire home is dusted, and vacuumed, and all left over construction debris is removed from the site of newly built homes. This kind of business is very inexpensive to promote, simply set up presentation appointments with property developers and contractors in your community and explain why they will benefit from your services.

217) Duct Cleaning Service- This business venture is the cleaning of furnaces and air conditioner ducts. The duct cleaning materials are relatively inexpensive and don't require a great deal of special skills and knowledge. Which makes this a very attractive business opportunity? Establishing a working relationship such as with heating contractors, real estate agents, and property management companies this can go a long way in establishing a client base.

218) Storm Window Installation Storage- This business opportunity provides home owners with services of installing storm windows. You could earn a seasonal income of $15 to $25 per hour provided you supply homeowners with optional window repair, and cleaning as an additional service. You'll need basic tools such as hammers, screw drivers, and a few ladders.

219) Blind Cleaning Service- If you chose to start a blind cleaning service, you will need to remove and label your customers blinds, and transport them to a central cleaning location. The second options would clean your customer's blinds on site, using cleaning tanks that can be mounted on a trailer or a truck. Clean all you client's blinds by hand washing them using cleaning agents and dusters. You can market your services through fliers to property management companies and at home trade shows as well as in the community.

220) House Cleaning Service- To start a business of this nature is relatively easy and inexpensive. Currently house cleaning rates are in the range of $25 to$50 per hour, the key to building up your house cleaning staff is to be very good at finding them work. You will need to market your business to home owners, property managers, and by the way of a website. Let your clients know that you and your staff is reliable, well trained, and bonded. Once you get the ball rolling this can be a very lucrative business venture.

221) Air Conditioning Service- Simply pre- market the service you offer, and build up your client base. Design a well put together presentation package outlining your special skills and abilities, along with your service rates, then, past out your package to potential clients such as residential and commercial management companies.

222) Pest Control Service- You will need licenses to start a business as a pest control service. A pest control service can be very profitable. There are several types of pest control services, such as insect and rodent control, or you could specialize in all the above areas. There are several methods being used to control pest such as chemical based sprays, and organic based spray. Overall you could generate over $75,000 per year.

223) Home Inspection Service- A home inspection service will require that you have construction experience. You will also have to invest time and money to become a certified home inspector. A home inspector makes sure that homes do not have major mechanical & structural problems. Home inspectors rate range from $150 for a small residential home, to more than $1,000 for larger homes and commercial buildings. A business like this can be managed from a home base office.

224) Window Washing Service- To start a business as a window washing service, you will have a low start up investment cost. No skills required, no experience, flexible hours, no inventory, you can offer interior and exterior window cleaning, potential sales in excess of $50,000 per year. Marketing your service will be very simple, you could secure corporate contracts and don't forget residential and commercial properties. Access to the strata corporation market can be gained by establishing contact with property management firms. These types of firms can indicate when and where the window business contract becomes available. Whether your business washing windows are large or small both can be very profitable, your services can

easily earn an income in excess of $50,000 per year after business expenses.

225) Garden Tilling Service-A garden tilling service is very inexpensive to operate. The equipment to start a business of this nature can be new or used or even rented. The startup cost is low, market and distribute fliers, and door hangers throughout your community promoting your service. You can earn a seasonal income of $20 to $50 per hour; you can also add an additional service by selling soil as well.

226) Christmas Light Installation- You can provide potential clients with Christmas light installation services, as well as taking the Christmas lights down after Christmas. This business could generate an extra income for you at least a few thousand dollars per year. You could also buy Christmas decorations wholesale and sell them for an additional income.

227) Carpet Cleaning Service- A carpet cleaning service is a great business venture, here's a list of reasons why? low investment, a proven customer demand, great profit potential, no inventory, home based, growth potential, no skills required, flexible business hours, minimal operating overhead. To market your service print and distribute coupon featuring a free carpet cleaning offer, you can also market your services to residential and commercial marketing firms, you can also make more money if you are able to clean all kinds of carpets.

228) Wireless Installation and Home Computer Network Services- More and more homes are utilizing wireless internet connections. The key is to be able to set the best locations in the home for wireless transmission, and know how to install the wireless routers, and adapters, and you must also know how to co figurate the system. You'll also need to know how to network home computers for maximum use.

229) Import/ Export Micro Guide- A business of this nature will require a great amount of research, supply and demand research will establish the demand for a product, legal requirements learn the laws, rules and regulations aspect of the industry as well as in the country you plan to do business. Contacts and alliances never overlook the importance of good contacts. Transportation, how will you transport your product, profitability, your business must be able to generate profit I order to stay in business.

230) Import Agent- If you have numerous business contacts in North American, you could become an import agent. A import agent represents products from foreign countries and works as a middle man to get their products distributed to wholesalers and retailers. The key to success is having the ability to build a business contact base; a good starting point is to join the WTO (World Trade Organization)

231) Clothing- The key to importing and exporting is to secure exclusive and unique apparel products that will have market appeal. The internet can be used as a research tool, seek small independent clothing manufactures from around the world and contact them concerning their product.

232) Food- Transporting food and plant from foreign countries there are strict rules and regulations and health codes. You will need to research carefully what you can and cannot send abroad, or import from other countries.

233) How To Books- How to book, tapes and software can retail for as much as $50 and cost as little as $3 each if bought wholesale, and this is what makes how to books, tapes, and software such great mail order products. How to books are related to business, relationships, health and fitness, self improvement, child raising, arts and crafts, a catalog can easily be produced featuring many titles on these subjects. And with purchase mailing, fax, email list you can be in the mail ordering businesses and filling customer's orders in a matter of weeks.

234) Home Schooling- if you have a teaching or educational background this is a great opportunity. You can start a consulting business that assists parents in establishing a home schooling educational program for their children. The program can be designed to help meet the educational needs of children of various ages, and stages of development as well as features

subject teaching, educational field trips, recreating social interaction activities.

235) Stop Smoking Clinics- Smokers often need guidance, assistance of nicotine patches, gums, and pills, start a stop smoking clinic or counseling service it's not difficult. The classes can be conducted in a group format, or a one on one in home consulting basis. You would need to develop a course manual, "The Guide to Stop Smoking," the guide can be the basis of the stop smoking program that you can offer to your clients.

236) River Rescue Instruction- To start a business of this nature you will need to secure a river rescue instruction certificate. Which can be gain by successfully completing a practical written exam, you'll also need equipment such as throw bags, ropes, safety harnesses, to conduct the instructional course. Most equipment is available for purchase at recreational outdoor retailers. Your potential client base will include the fire department, police, sports clubs, organizations, and fisherman.

237) Golf Instruction- If you have golf expertise you could start a business that teaches clients how to play golf, or how to improve their game, the business can be started with a small capital investment and managed from a home base. Golf pros charge between the price ranges of $40 to $200 per hour for a lesson. If you charge $100 for a one hour lesson, you might offer five lessons for $425 the profit potential is through the roof.

238) Truck Driving School- You must first acquire a special drivers permit or endorsement, starting a truck driving school requires a very large investment to establish and operate this business. However the potential profits are great, a truck driving course cost as much as $3,000 per student. You could generate extra income by providing transportation companies a refresher course for their employee. This opportunity is best served by a former truck driver who is up to date on the latest information that will approach the written test and road test. You should also know all the current laws & regulations that apply to truck driving.

239) Acting Class Private lessons- This is a very inexpensive business venture to establish, but the income potential is outstanding, if you are well trained in the field of acting, training classes and seminars could be held on an independent basis or be provided to students in conjunction with community programs, or after school programs. You could look into stage productions at the end of 8, 10, 12 week class period, Additional cash could be made by selling the videos of the final class performance & teach those interested in learning more on a private lesson basis.

240) Photograph Course- You could start a course that provide students in both traditional print and digital imaging format and you could also work from a home base, one marketing method would be to approach retailers that sell cameras and offer a free two hour photo course for their customers that purchase cameras. This type of free promotion is to have a large percentage of the students who take advantage of the free

course to sign up for an extended photograph course and training on a paid basis.

241) Cooking Class- you could start a cooking class on a shoestring budget and generate a yearly income of $4,000, you could also work from a home base once you secure the necessary zoning and licensing. You could also establish joint ventures with retailers that sell cooking ware, house ware or a restaurant. This option draws people into the establishment, plus they will get free advertising, your start up cost in minimal, capitalize on an existing client base, share overhead cost, and joint venture profit potentials are unlimited.

242) Gardening Class- You could conduct this class from a home base teaching how to garden classes, establish a working relationship with a local gardening center that can refer your classes to their clients, writing and publishing a garden new letter featuring local gardens and gardeners. Gardening tips are also a great way to increase business and revenues and profits. Try to secure at least 20 clients per week, each paying $50 for the garden instruction course, your result in a one year should be around $50,000

243) Home Renovation Classes- Starting a business teaching home renovation skills and techniques, the first is to establish an independent and charge students a fee to learn a specific home renovation trade such as how to pain, the second approach is to build a working relationship or joint venture with

local building and home centers, The classes can be free, you could capitalize o the building centers existing customers as a quick method to attract students.

244) Flying School- If you're considering starting a flying school as a business venture there are a lot of hurdles to overcome, both financial and regulatory. Small airplanes and pilots are in high demand for the film industry. And are commanding as much as $1500 per day to start, starting a flying school includes securing the availability of a small airport, and liability insurance, equipment and marketing your lessons. Experience flier pilots can make good money once they get the business off the ground.

245) Dog Training Classes- To launch a dog training business, you must first become certified, the classes can be conducted from a fixed location or a mobile business or you could conduct the training from the client's home, one on one training are in the range of $30 to $40 per hour. Selling books on training and obedience topics to clients as well as specialty dog foods, and equipment such as leeches and collars can also generate extra income.

246) Dance Studio- If you are not a dancer a professional can be hired on a part time basis, you can increase revenues and profits by videotaping the instruction classes and sell them by mail order, or the internet or both. For extra income you can also offer private lessons, the potential to create a six figure

income by operating a dance studio is very achievable providing sound business and marketing are provided. You will also need to locate a good location plus liability insurance

247) Educational Tutor- A business like this can be operated on a mobile basis or from a home base, By networking with school personnel, and parent teacher associations and advertising locally current rates from professional tutors vary from a low $25 per hour to $90 per hour depending on the course material and if you are good. Word can spread quickly attracting more clients.

248) Auto Maintenance Course- Start a business that teaches students how to do general maintenance on cars and trucks, the course can be conducted in association with a community or educational facility or a community college. Lease a small working and training space, providing you secure 10 to 20 paying clients per week, for a 3 hour auto maintenance course and charge $50 each you could generate an earning income of $2,000 per month.

249) Jewelry Making Instruction- If you are interested in starting a jewelry making instruction business, build up an alliance with craft stores, retailers and community centers. You could also hold the instruction classes in your home. A mere four classes per week with 10 students paying $20 each will create business revenue in excess of $40,000 per year.

250) Fashion Design School- The first approach to starting a fashion design school that is recognized by fashion designers and manufacturers, a less costly and less complicated approach to starting the school would be to target students who have an interest in starting their own fashion label or clothing manufacturing business. This type of business is costly to establish, however the potential to generate a six figure yearly income is certainly attainable for a hard working entrepreneur.

251) Public Speaking Instruction- Starting an instructional business that specializes in training business owners, managers, and employees to become effective public speakers is a great new business venture. To set things in motion the best way to market this type of business of instruction, service is to design a complete marketing presentation and distribute the presentation to the most likely potential clients and include a CD and DVD. A good segment of the market to focus on is businesses and companies with medium to large scale forces. The training course can be conducted right at the client's location, aim to secure 3 clients per week. For a specialized half a day public speaking course and you will be on your way to earning $100,000 a year. Market such a course by wowing them with your expertise book short speaking engagements in which you discuss the power of being a good speaker in a well honed presentation. Private coaching before a major presentation can also generate additional income as can sell books, videos, and CD and DVD's.

252) Self Defense Training- This business opportunity will appeal to anyone with military, or police service background, providing you are qualified to teach self defense , an excellent income can be earned, you can conduct these classes on a one on one basis or at clients home, you can also hire qualified instructors to conduct the classes for you.

253) Sport Coach Training- There is a growing market for this kind of business on how to be better at a particular sport, the idea is to organize, market and conduct seminars for sports coaches with specialized management interaction and social responsibility. Themes to help train them to be better mentors and teachers, you can also enlist the service of a professional and motivational speaker, Hand out printed material on the subject they are teaching. The seminars can be marked directly to amateur sports associations, clubs, leagues, and organizations by direct mail campaign.

254) Adult Learning- To start an adult learning environment, advertise by distributing course directions widely with a short write up of the specific course offered hobbies, yoga, fitness, business classes, and the arts, are all very popular topics that can be taught in a 4 week course. You could also run numerous 1 night a week seminar, Start up cost will be minimal, student can sign up filling out an admissions form online or in a course booklet. Once you have set up a website for the adult learning course and have the class instruction you will be well on your way to earning unlimited potential.

255) Boxing Lessons- You could teach boxing lessons by setting up mats, or even a boxing ring in an established facility like a community center will provide you with such a place to run your classes, the pay rate will be from $10 to $15 per class. You can even set up classes in groups of 8 to 10 students. Before starting this business venture make sure you have liability insurance, and get certified as a boxing instructor.

256) CPR Lessons- You must be certified to teach a CPR course, you can rent space from hospitals, the YMCA, or even day care centers, churches, and community centers and teach this life saving course. Potential profits are unlimited and also check to make sure that the pay rate is for a call of this nature in your specific area.

257) Swimming Lessons & Water Safety- You could earn extra income by becoming a swimming instructor; once you mastered the skill yourself you can give individual or group lessons. You can set up 5 to 10 private lessons from $200 to $500 or charge less for group lessons, $300 for 6 lessons or $50 per lesson. You can teach 10 lessons per week and earn $25,000 for this side business.

258) Tennis Instructor- You could work out a deal with a court owner or director of a facility to teach tennis lessons, advertise by posting signs and posters everywhere they are permitted, and also do local advertising in order to be successful as a instructor. You must have a firm understanding of the game,

patience to work with people, and the ability to teach people, so hone your skills and you could have a successful tennis business.

259) Water Beds- starting a business venture that manufacture and sell water beds or parts of water beds such as liners, heaters, are available from numerous manufacturers on a wholesale basis, you simply design the frame and assemble the other parts to fit, you could sell directly to the consumer via placing advertisements in traditional mediums or sell the beds through the internet and at furniture shows.

260) Custom Picture Frames- Manufacture and wholesale custom designed picture frames; this is a great past time home base business. The more unique the material the more interesting the picture frames. Customers are always attracted to different one of kind products. Establish a wholesale account with photographic stores, photo finishing stores, gift shops and specialty shops.

261) Wooden Signs-To manufacture highly attractive and functional wooden signs first use a router to remove wood, and leave the message or words raised concave. The second method requires a design stencil and sandblasting equipment to remove the wood around the message in the words. Such signs are extremely popular with bed and breakfast lodges, lawyers, and accountants, doctors, and antique shops, gift shops and various other businesses high quality signs are selling at prices starting

at $500 each and up depending on the size and the type of wood used.

262) Mailboxes- To build custom design mailboxes, this can be a home based business with hours and a wage of $20 per hour offered. This business can be launched on an initial investment of less than $500 and operated on a part time, full time basis; the mailboxes can be sold wholesale or retail or on the weekend at the flea market or at a craft show. The profit potential could be in the range of $100,000 a year.

263) Parking Lot Line Painting- For a business like this potential customer include property owners, who require well marked parking and driving instruction painted on their parking lots, Also approach owners of newly constructed buildings and adjoining parking lots, the profit potential is whatever you want it to be for a business as lucrative as this one.

264) Snow Removal Service- You could generate an income of up to $30 per hour or more when this kind of service is in season. There are potential clients everywhere when it comes to removing snow. All you'll need is a shovel, or a snow blower, and a four wheel drive truck.

265) Fire Wood Delivery- The only requirements for a business like this is to purchase a truck capable of delivering the firewood, the least costly and quick way to establish is to simply

purchase split firewood in bulk and have it shipped to your yard or location. After this has been established you can deliver the firewood to customer in smaller quality.

266) Stump Removal Service- If you start a business removing tree stump the going rate is $35 to $50 per hour you could establish business with construction companies, landscaping companies, architects. Etc...

267) Patio Lighting- `The key to success in this business is to seek a manufacture of high quality lighting products and become the manufacture exclusive distributor and installer for their product, you can market to the end clients, you can also provide your service to architects, home builders, and patio contractors on a subcontract basis.

268) Tree Planting Service- Starting a tree planting service, you'll need to secure the tree planting contracts, be prepared to work hard and form crews of planting laborers. The common tree planting contract exceeds $100,000 in value.

269) Landscaping Service- Launching a landscaping service is a seasonal job. The business can be set in motion for less than $10,000, a lot of experience can be learned on the job, and the business will require that you have some past landscaping knowledge and skill and experience. Potential customers

include property owners, residential property owners, and commercial property owners.

270) Garden Planning Service- If you have gardening skills and basic marketing skills. A business like this could require much investment capital, or you could manage this business from a home base. Your job function would be to supply your clients with required seed, plants, and gardening equipment. Do more research to find out more on the subject of gardening?

271) Bob cat Service- A bobcat service is an outstanding business venture, the key to the benefits of running a bobcat service includes snow removal, top soil moving tree planting, excavating earth, digging potholes, and removing tree stumps, the profit potential for this service range from $50 to $80 per hour/ $350 to $500 per day. Securing 25 hours of work can produce business revenues in excess of $10,000 per year.

272) Tree Trimming and Removal Service- The equipment you'll need is a ladder, a truck, safety gear, chain saws, and pruning shears, design and distribute promotional flyers, placing advertisements for your service in newspapers, and in the yellow pages as well as competing for tree trimming and removal contracts and tenders.

273) Chain Saw Service- This service can be marketed directly to homeowners by placing a small classified ad in the newspaper.

You can also provide service on a sub contract basis. This is a great low cost business that can produce a part time income of $25 per hour. You will need to establish liability insurance also take all the necessary safety precautions.

274) Fishing Bait Sales- This is a very profitable business stocking and selling fishing bait, everything from Mina and Dow worms, and leeches, carefully plan, do your research your business can be started from home under the right conditions or you could set up the business in a rental location.

275) RV washing Service- To start this type of business venture simply establish alliances with overnight RV parks and campgrounds. You should have no problem charging in the range of $15 to $25 to wash the exterior of an average size RV and the time frame of 30 minutes.

276) Full Car Wash- setting up a car wash business can be costly, but bi profits can also be made. Hand drying, interior cleaning, and other low cost quality service features. You can also offer a detailing service is you have the experience profit potential range from $15 to $35 per hour depending on the service.

277) Commercial Lawn Care- You could start a business in commercial lawn care, cutting grass for apartment complexes, medical facilities, office parks, and shopping malls, starting cost

would be under $15,000, but also make sure you get the proper licensing and liability insurance before starting your business.

278) Golf Course Maintenance- landscaping golf courses require unique care, before even considering this service you would need to work for a golf course maintenance service, for a year or two because this kind of business requires a lot of experience.

279) Doggie Wash & Salon- A business like this can be established in a retail location, distribute free doggie wash coupons throughout your community letting potential clients know where you are located, set up cost should be under $19,000 to start this business and profit potential can be excellent.

280) Mobile Dog Wash Service- Promote your doggie wash service with promotional fliers and display at pet retailers, vets, and the local ASPCA generate revenues for a charity and you can provide the service for a 50% split of revenues generated.

281) Dog Walk Service- Once you spread the word about your dog walk service it should not take long to establish a base of 20 to 30 regular clients. $12 per dog per day or a weekly discount of $55 for 5 days, you could make over $1, 375 per week or more than $10,000 per year.

282) Custom Collar and Leech Manufacture- This has proven to be a very profitable business venture, you could even turn it into a full time or part time business. The only requirement to set this business in motion is sewing machine, and the ability to sew. Market your product after you've done the research, at dog shows, pet stores, the vets and wherever there is a market for doggie products.

283) Pet Grooming- This business is very inexpensive to start, and can be extremely profitable. Grooming a medium sized dog range from $30 to $100 per visit, additionally income can be gained for free grooming service by selling pet grooming products.

284) House Safety Pets- Starting a business that focus on securing the household to prevent pet injury, can be very rewarding, distribute fliers about your services to a pet related businesses, such as the ASPCA, pet food stores, the vets, and doggie and cat clinics. You could also charge clients an in home fee for pet safety consulting.

285) Pet Day Care-This should not be confused with a kennel service; this is a pet day care center. To market this business simply form an alliance with all pet related stores, owners, and vets, start up cost shouldn't be over $39,000, but profit potential for doggie day care are from $14 to $20 per day.

286)) Pet Emergency Kits- Starting a business that manufacture, assemble, and wholesale emergency kits for pets doesn't require experience, the key to success is to make the packaging effective. As well as establishing as many wholesale accounts as possible.

287) Pet Food Store-Open a store that sells all kinds of pet food if you want to break into this business and be a success, including organic pet foods, maintain annual sales of $200,000 and 100 % markup will create annual gross profits of $100,000 yearly and sky will be the limit for your pet food store.

288) Pet Food Bowls- Design, manufacture, and wholesale pet food bowls, this would be a great home base business to start. The key to success with this kind of business is for the bowls to be interesting, construction and sale could easily top $1,000 a day if done right so do your research.

289) Pet Name Books- Pet name books could focus on one particular type of pet, such as cats or dogs or you could feature historical pet names, or celebrity pet names. You would need to research to look up publishing houses that might print such a book, the current commission or royalty rate is typically 4 to 8 % of the gross total value of books sold.

290) Pet Travel Kits- Starting a business that package pet travel kits, you could start out as a home base business. The kits can include things such as water, sunshade products, treats and the list goes on to how many products you could include in your kits. The kits can be sold on a wholesale or retail basis of both. Potential profits are greater than $25,000 per year, selling the kits at $5 each will generate an income of $25,000

291) Pet Grooming Kits- Starting a business that design pet grooming kits, and package and wholesale pet grooming kits. That can be sold retail or wholesale or both. This type of business concept has the potential to gross millions of dollars in annual sales do the research and sees which way you would like your pet grooming business to go.

292) Pet Breeder- Chances are you will have a very profitable and rewarding business. Starting a pet breeding business includes qualification, business location, registration, association membership and marketing skill and abilities after this sky's are the limit. Do the research to find out what breed of animal you would like to breed.

293) Pet Mats- Selling pet mat for dogs and cats can be a great business venture. The mats can be sold directly to consumers or via specialty stores, or you could sell them at the weekend flea market, you could generate sales of up to $1,000 a day for this lucrative business idea.

294) Pet Sitting- There is excellent money to be made sitting for pets, especially for those who love pets. A pet sitter make typically from $10 to $20 per visit. Therefore, if you have 10 sitters each making 20 visits per week or a total of 2000 pets visit per week, you could collect $4,000 of which you will make $1,000 per week.

295) Doggie Clothing- Sweaters, rain wear, hats, even goggles, are all part of a doggie ensemble. You will need sewing equipment, creative marketing, and a website to show your goods, the profit potential is excellent for this business venture.

296) Gourmet Style Dog Treats- Healthy dog biscuit made from the finest ingredients are all you'll need and some healthy gourmet recipes, biscuit molds, unique packages and a dynamite marketing plan and you're on your way to a very profitable business venture that can make you rich.

297) Pet Transportation- Pet transportation services are in popular demand. Clients want to trust that you can move pets safely and comfortably. Start up cost can be high since you'll need a vehicle. But with a specialized service like this you could generate a hefty income.

298) Real Estate Photo Service- This can be a very inexperienced home base business, the best way to market a real estate photo service is to arrange appointments with real

estate agents and present a portfolio and hones buildings and property's that you have photographed. Photographing produce sells in excess of $50,000 per year.

299) Video Editing Service- a video editing service can easily be operated from a home base, studio and the business can focus both on video and editing. The market your business through camcorder retailer and on your website like all business opportunities, hard work, research and practice and planning can pay off.

300) Photograph business that provide specialty calendars for clients in five away to valuable customers, as a business promotion, this business is very easy to market, design sample calendars and set appointment to present the product to local companies.

301) Personal Postcards- Get started making your own personal postcards, with computer equipment, software and digital camera the main business requirement you'll need to get the ball rolling. Excellent location is always good, including tourist attractions, amusement parks, sport and fitness, etc....

302) Wedding Photographer- It would be nice to start a wedding photograph business or an agency representing wedding photographers, once you are ready to strike out on your own. Market your service to wedding planner's caterers,

and on your website. Revenues can be generated by charging the photographers a yearly fee to be listed and from advertising revenues from related business such as wedding planners and caterers.

303) Holiday Greeting Cards- If you want to start a business of this nature, selling holiday greeting cards,, get them rolling in August and September, because it will take them time to get printed and shipped, this is a great home base business opportunity that can generate a profit of $20,000 or more each year.

304) Home Photographer- If you would like to use your photography skills to start a home business. Simply photograph homes in your community, during Christmas, sunset and storms, picture taken at this time are excellent photos. Potential profits for this kind of business are $10,000 per year and up.

305) Photo I.D. Badges- To start a business making photo I.D. badges typically photo I.D. badges can cost you less than $3.00 each to make, but you can sell them for $6.00 or 47.00 each, and of course you can also make them in bulk orders of 25 and more.

306) Property Management- As a property manager, you duties will include handling trades people, and conduct repairs on the building or structure and reply to tenant and owner inquires,

leasing vacant apartments, negotiate lease forms and details you will need to know landlord and tenant legal rights.

307) Commercial Leasing Agent- To do this as a business, you will need to educate yourself out the laws in commercial property and estate leases and contracts. A business if this nature can be start up for less than $10,000 and can return as much as $100,000 per year income you will need to research the topic as well as check local regulation of the legalities before becoming a leasing agent.

308) Mini Storage Center- Business owners require storage space for products, displays, and equipment. You will need to find enough storage footage and buy facility insurance; however the income that can be earned from a well established storage business can exceed $150,000 a year and more.

309) House Tours- This business can include historic homes, land marks, and celebrity homes. The business can also go viral giving clients a glimpse of these homes via your website. If you could get 200 clients per week, paying $10 for the tour you will generate revenue of $100,000 per year.

310) Mortgage Broker- you will need to get proper certificates and take a course on mortgages to break into this business, study up on different types of mortgages, it's important to know what a balloon mortgage is, ARMS, fixed rate mortgages, the

current interest rates, point and credits reports, This is a very profitable business to launch just do the required research

311) Paint Ball Game- This business venture is quite simple, people pay a fee to be transported to paint ball game site locations, market the game by going to large groups, these are ideal candidates and you could also promote your game site through corporations, schools, and clubs, and sport associations.

312) Mobile Rock Climbing- A mobile rock climbing wall that is mounted on a trailer and designed for fast assembling and dismantling convenience can be used for the following instruction, fun, business promotions, and other profit potential excitement.

313) Camp Ground- To start a campground operation or a seasonal campground with tent only, trailer access, and motor homes, of course you will need to be very knowledgeable about camping in order to promote your campground, in hunting magazines, fishing and sport magazine once you research how to market your camp ground income potential will generate.

314) Horse Back Riding- Starting a horseback riding, training, and boarding facility this will require a enormous capital investment, if you're a horse fanatic you'll be able to pull it off. You could rent horses to ride by the hour, eventually you'll be

able to own your own small stable, and the profit potential for this business is astronomical.

315) Hiking Guide Book- You could write your own hiking guide book, the book can include local trails, hiking areas, and information on how to get to the trails, and what to look for, and what to watch out for while hiking in certain areas. The guide can be sold through local retailers and also it can be published on a yearly basis to keep the revenues coming in.

316) Water Ski Tours- If you're looking for a business where you can enjoy the sun, surf and sand purchase a boat and water ski equipment and charge beach goers and vacationers fees for 15 to 20 minutes of water skiing up and down the beach, a business license is required and a boat and liability insurance.

317) Baseball Batting Cage- Start a batting cage business can be quite lucrative and fun, the facility will generate enough business on its own to pay for the land or indoor family center. You will definitely need liability insurance. You can market your batting cage business to the little league, softball leagues, high school and college teams; you can make extra money by selling batting gloves, photos taken while a batter swing this is a profitable business.

318) Used Mattress Sale- If you would like to start a recycling business, this one can be started for a very small investment,

used mattresses can be bought and re-sold, a business of this nature can generate a great profit of $18,000 each year.

319) Flea Market Host- A flea market has a large indoor and outdoor area into smaller subsections, and rent those spaces on a weekly basis, or monthly and yearly basis as well. You could advertise your flea market in newspapers, fliers, and via the internet. This is a great business opportunity that has great income potential and can generate large profit.

320) Secondhand Bookstore- Opening a retail store that sells second hand books and publications is a great business venture, when selling books the price should be around 25 to 50 % of original retail value, the profit potential is outstanding for this business venture do your research.

321) Cardboard Boxes- Starting a cardboard box collection and recycling business is a very easy venture, you could collect boxes from retailers, grocery stores, manufactures, and sell them to the local or state cardboard box recycling facility. Cardboard boxes are a commodity you should generate a part time income of $1,000 per month.

322) Tires- Starting a tire recycle business takes time and money, and lot so creative development. A used tire business stands a better chance of being successful and rewarding. This is

a good business venture just do the research to find out about how to recycle used tires.

323) Recycle Kitchen Cabinets- Finding a good supply of second hand kitchen cabinets for re-sell is very simple, actually you can get this cabinet for free, simply by agreeing to pick them up and remove them from a site. By placing ads in the penny saver publication or the newspaper you could earn a few thousand dollars each year.

324) Paper Recycling- Collecting piles of paper from homes and businesses and selling them to a recycle plant in your area can add up to a great some of money, paper recycling has been known to reach the amount of $100,000 income mark for a year of hard work.

325) Power Tools- By purchasing good quality commercial power tools, just design an informational brochure listening your power tools description. The rental listing can be distributed to local construction and renovation companies. The investment capital to start this kind of business venture range from $20,000 to $25,000, and your profit potential

326) Karaoke Machine- A karaoke machine can be rented by nightclubs, disc jockeys, and event and wedding planners, the startup cost on your initial investment should be $2,000 for a good karaoke machine, you could rent the machine for $100 to

$150 per day part time your profit potential will range from $12,000 per year.

327) Pool Tables- Starting a pool table rental business, renting pool tables for parties, corporate gatherings, and conventions. The startup cost of a business venture like this a complete pool table package would retail for $1,500 to $3,000, for good quality pool tables and equipment can be purchased for half that cost.

328) Office Equipment- Filing cabinets, desk, chairs, telephone systems, copiers and computers are needed in order for a business to function, to start a business venture that rent office equipment and furniture, new and used would be in the range of $ 30,000 to $50,000, your profit potential will gross $1,500 month.

329) Casino Equipment- Renting casino equipment for charity events, fundraising events, and business promotional events to establish your rental service this will be costly $50,000 to $100,000 but the profit potential will be greater depending on the business venture.

330) Fencing- Renting portable fences to construction companies, event planners, can be operated from a home base, start up investment capital range from $15,000 to $30,000. The income potential is determined by the total number of linear feet per job, 370) Boating- Renting boats is a very lucrative

business to establish, design colorful brochures and distribute them to hotel, motels, and tourist attractions. Small second hand boats, sells in the range of $2,500 to $5,000 each, a initial investment of $15,000 will get your business floating, you can rent your small boats for at least $100 a day.

331) Portable Signs- Starting a portable sign rental business will allow you to cash in on retailers seeking to promote their businesses, start up investment range from $10,000 to $15,000, not to mention a sign rent for $75 a day, and $150 per week. You can generate serious cash from this venture.

332) Bouncy Houses- portable, inflatable, bouncy houses for children's birthday parties, fundraising events, or a tourist high traffic area, or a community gathering either way you could charge parents $3 to $4 for their children to spend 10 minutes in your bounce house. To purchase a large bouncy house as an initial investment would be around$1,400, and rent the unit out of $200 for a couple of hours, you would generate an income of $4,000 by weekly especially in the spring and summer months.

333) Go Carts- An investment in a go cart track could range from $250,000 and up. But a well established go cart track can provide sizable profits that could surplus $100,000 a year, but that's only if your go kart track is located in the right area.

334) Bicycles-You could rent out bicycles for tourist and vacationers, people will rent bicycles to ride along the boardwalk, or in the park. You could start a bicycle rental business for around $7,000 to $15,000 for 15 to 25 bicycles and don't forget to provide helmets for your customers. Bike usually rent for $15 to $20 an hour depending on the demand.

335) Uniforms- A uniform rental business can supply clothing for just about any event, butlers, domestic uniforms, lab coats, medical clothing, chefs, food servers, uniforms need for short term use only. Put together a brochure, or catalog, or advertise on your website and make sure you stock up heavily on a variety of sizes.

336) Sunglasses- Selling sunglasses is a very inexpensive business to start with excellent profit potential. You can sell the glasses from home via the internet, or at the mall, the beach, or at the flea market on the weekend.

337) Gift baskets- You could assemble gift baskets by simply selecting food, flowers, personal health items, and arrange them in a attractive wicker basket. The secret to success is to own and operate a gift basket service; gift basket is in the price range of $30 to $40 you could achieve an income profit of $150,000 a year especially during special occasion.

338) Airbrush Helmet- This unique business venture can be lucrative only if your air brush the helmets on site. Baseball, hockey, football, bicycle, motorcycle helmets, if you feature binders with pictures and images for clients to choose from, your helmets can sell for $25 and up depending on the design. A business like this can generate sales in the millions.

339) Dollar Discount Store-To make a dollar discount store work, you will find the perfect location and sells product such as inexpensive items that retail for less than $5 kitchen products, toys, household products, less expensive version of popular name brand items you will also need to sell these items in volume to make a business like this work.

340) Janitorial Supplies- Starting a janitorial business selling janitorial supplies to companies like government agencies, organizations, educational institutions, and other associations are a very lucrative business venture, the product is normally sold for no more than 10 to 20 percent over cost.

341) News Stand- Starting a news stand requires getting in touch with one or more distributors that carry just about every kind of magazine, publication and newspaper you can image. By having a few specialty publications you could draw clients to your newsstand, seek out a location where you can stay in touch with your customers like near the train station, bus stops, hospitals, and the airport.

342) Wholesaler- There are many types of products that are sold on a wholesale basis, food, computers, clothing, telecommunication services, starting this type of business you would have to do massive research to make sure you're getting good deals.

343) Bumper Stickers- Here are 5 steps to establishing a business venture selling bumper sticker, a business like this could put you on the path to financial freedom, first you must hire an artist to design the bumper stickers, design a (pop) point of purchase display that can hold 20 to 200 bumper stickers, establish wholesale accounts with retailers, establish accounts with national multi unit retailers, establish a website that features thousand of different bumper sticker designs. Your bumper stickers can be printed in mass quantity for less than $0.10 each and sold for more than $4 each

344) Video Game Store-With a good location and all the latest titles, selling games, game consoles, controllers, and accessories will increase your profit base you can also add a website to sell your games and a newsletter and anything else that has to do with the gaming industry.

345) Neon Signs- To start a neon sign business it will cost you around $10,000, a business that design and sell neon signs the profit potential can easily exceed $100,000 per year. Utilize a computer and design software, and once the design is

completed build a presentation to present to your clients it that easy.

346) Vacuum Cleaner Sales- A vacuum cleaner sales and repair business is a great small business venture if you establish exclusive sales, service and distribution and expand the product line to sale built in vacuums can greatly increase your revenues and profit. Look up and do the research on the product line since there are many manufacturers that sale different style vacuums

347) Greeting Card Store- This is a lucrative market that can make you rich, you can start out with a good retail location and service local customers, by purchasing greeting cards in bulk on a wholesale basis, you could also carry paper plates, party plates, balloons and other party favorites.

348) Ladies Shoes- Boots, heels, flats, tennis shoes, pumps, sandals, women's shoes are very profitable, all you basically need is a good location to sell your wares, opening a shoe store can cost anywhere from $1,500 to $450,000 just to open. Or you could become a representative for a manufacture of shoes cutting costs out completely. Sale your shoes by way of a website, a booth at the local mall profit potential are unlimited.

349) Cell phone Accessories- To start a business selling cell phone accessories from a booth in the mall, or at a fair, a small shop, shared space with other retailers, or from your website, car adapters, head sets, cell phone covers, chargers, holsters, and external antenna. Just look for wholesalers with the latest trends.

350) Wireless Store- You can cash in on a growing technology industry, selling Sirius radios, satellite networks, equipment, laptops, Bluetooth's, products, you can set up a small store front location or a website or both for an initial investment of $75,000 you could launch this business with sufficient inventory.

351) Glass Shop- Windows, tabletops, mirrors, operating this kind of specialty business requires experience in glass cutting, and glass installation technique or glazing. There are various types of glass installation and your business could focus on one. A venture like this can be very costly to establish. But you can easily generate profit of $75,000 per year.

352) Hobby Shop- model trains, puzzles, games, launching a hobby shop can put you on the path to financial freedom. The possibilities are endless, the investment required to open a hobby shop will depend on the way the shop is set up. Do the research and familiarize yourself with as many popular hobbies as possible.

353) Fire Safety Ladders- A business that manufacture, sells and installs safety ladder for residents, and commercial businesses has the potential to generate profits of $250,000 a year. Due to an almost unlimited market for the product, the investment to start a business such as this can easily exceed $100,000

354) Window Security Bars- Starting a business that manufacture and install window security bars can be sold to residential homeowners as well as commercial property and business owners. You will need an invest of $20,000 to $25,000 to establish a small to medium manufacturing facility, but the profit potential could exceed yearly sales of $300,000

355) Home Alarm Sales- To start a business that sell and install alarms to residential and commercial applications, you would need to market your alarms by advertising and distributing fliers, or you can advertise on your website and at home shows.

356) Body Guard Security Service- Starting a business like this requires a great deal of planning and research. Bodyguards can earn as much as $1,000 a day a few days per week, generating business sales in excess of $200,000 per year. You would have to make sure you meet the needs of your clients' ad have signed contracts that are very specific in what you can and won't do, this will limit the potential liability claims that can arise from an overzealous bodyguard.

357) Surveillance Equipment-video cameras, emergency service scanners, night vision glasses, and other types of surveillance equipment, starting a business that retails these surveillance devices is very easy to do. Locate manufactures of surveillance equipment and purchase the equipment on a wholesale basis. Advertise in newspapers, trade publications, for catalog ordering, enabling customers to receive your surveillance equipment by mail or establish a website the profit potential for this type of business is out of this world.

358) Guard Dogs- To start this type of business you must have trained dogs, either experience or affiliated with a dog trainer, You'll also have to have a suitable location, and dog rental rates are in the range of $40 to $60 per eight hours including delivery and pick up. You will need liability insurance, licensing, depending on the region.

359) Locksmith- You must be certified to start a locksmith business; instructional training shouldn't take more than one year to complete. This is proving to be a profitable business venture within come potential ranging from $20,000 to $80,000 a year.

360) Security Safety Mirrors- This is an unlimited market and a great business venture. The only requirement you'll need for this business is a step ladder or a couple of step ladders and a cordless drill. No skill required, anyone can install security

mirrors, start up investment is from $3,000 to $10,000, and the profit potential is over $4,000 per month.

361) Personal Security Products- Security product such as mace, pepper spray, stun guns, whistles, personal alarms, can all be purchased wholesale from over one hundred different manufacturers and wholesalers. You can sell and distribute the personal security products through mail order or via the internet on your website, or retail sales, or from sales booths at the mall make sure all the products you're going to list are legal in your area.

362) Auto Alarm Sales, Installation- This is a good business venture of your establish alliance with used car dealers, this is a fabulous way to activate this security business. Car dealer can offer their clients optional installation. Auto alarm sales and installation range from $25,000 to $50,000 to establish a business of this nature.

363) Life Guard Service- A life guard service provides highly trained, skilled life guards, to pools and beaches and around the community, cities, and states, This can certainly be a home base business with low start up cost, and a potentially successful business venture. But first you must become skilled and certified to handle a life guard's responsibility.

364) School Security Consultant- Market your services to the local schools and the school board and then move your services to private schools in your area, by selling your knowledge and expertise. You can operate this type of business from a home base, and bill your clients $60 or more per hour to help examine and analyze the current state of the school. By working with the school personnel and evaluating the infrastructure of the facility.

365) Community and Development Patrol- This is a marvelous opportunity to launch your own community and development patrol business, many developments have swimming pools, community centers, playgrounds, if you have a law enforcement background this could be the business for you. That you can launch for more than $1,000 once you have obtained the necessary licensing you can seek out clients, from a business like this you can secure profits of $50,000 a year or more depending on the location.

366)) Dry Cleaner Delivery Service- To start a business like this build an alliance with commercial dry cleaners, and negotiate the lowest possible per item dry cleaner rate. After this has been established you would need to solicit clients such as companies with uniforms, professional officers, government and nonprofit organizations.

367) Office Moving Service- To start a moving service like this one you could market through company management companies, and directly to business owners via brochures and networking at business association functions. You will need to get liability insurance and check to see if a mover's license is required in your community.

368) Body Piercing- Starting this kind of business does require experience, or an inexperienced staff plus liability insurance. You can start a body piercing business for a very small investment. And can easily generate weekly sales in excess of $1,000

369) Reunion Planner- To start a reunion planner service, you will need to acquire numerous old high school and college yearbooks, start a direct mail inquire about student interested in a reunion, you can charge $60 per individual or $100 per couple. Do the research and customize themes, you can easily generate a part time income of $12,000 to $15,000 per year.

370) Networking Club- Starting a network club in your community is a perfect way to be self employed and make large numbers of new and valuable business contact, network clubs are a perfect choice for a new business tart up.

371) Telephone On Hold Advertising- For the business concept you create an on hold advertising message for your clients hire a professional voice person to record the message. The profit potential for this kind of service is excellent.

372) Packing Service- You can start your own packing service for very little money, generally for his type of service you would charge on a per hour rate, or for the entire job a flat rate. Charge at least $20 per hour for your services.

373) Commercial Door Maintenance Service- Starting a commercial door maintenance route may be your opportunity to earn an excess of $100,000 per year, with a minimal door closure and pivots, replacing automatic doors, lubricating pivots, and concealing hinges, current service rate start in the range of $40 to $60 per hour.

374) Coat Check Service-Providing a coat check service for one social function per week, and charging only $125 for the service will earn you an additional $6,500 per year. Clients can include weddings, event planners, catering companies, tradeshows, and seminar organizations; with this business you can establish a good part time income.

375) Nail Salon- To run a nail salon there are numerous approaches, first become established in a fixed location, or partner with an existing business, so, start a mobile nail salon

that travels to the clients' houses, But you must possess the proper credentials to get started, once established a nail salon can generate profits in the range of $40,000 per year.

376) Distribution Warehouse- This can be a nice home base business venture and internet service for distribution warehouse services. Your duties will include acting a shipping and receiving agent for as many as twenty to thirty companies. A business like this requires is a great deal of investment capital and research.

377) Mailbox Center- this is an easy business venture, it requires no skill, or experience the main requirements would be a small retail store front, a few pieces of office furniture, equipment such as a high speed photocopier, personal computer, a fax, and a scanner. You can act as a drop off or pick up depot for courier companies. If you put in the work you can make this a booming business.

378) Showroom Design- A showroom must be visibly appealing, and customer friendly. You can utilize your creative talents; a showroom doesn't require a lot of capital to start. However the experience and designer knowledge is required and order to succeed. Other duties would include supplying your clients with window display service, renting props for showroom displays, and special sales for promotional events. 419) Limo Service- You can easily put yourself in the $300,000 start up range, plus you will have to hire a dispatcher unless you plan on doing this

yourself, you'll also need new cars every three to four years in order to stay competitive, and you will have to hire someone reliable to drive your clients to their destination. Your duties would be to supply corporate clients with limo service such as weddings, proms, parties, plus airport runs can make for a very lucrative service.

379) Auction Buyer Service- A business as an auction buyer start up cost will really be interesting to those who have skills and abilities, such as an art appraiser, antique car appraiser, the more specialized you make your service the better the chances to eliminate the competition and better chances to increase your auction buyer service revenues and profits.

380) Hair Dresser- If you have a hairdressing license starting your own hairdressing business can be a great way to make a hefty profit. You can open as a mall salon in a good location, or go into business with another entrepreneur, or start a mobile business doing hair of people who cannot travel easily, you can also market yourself to the elderly & disable clients, and profit potential can easily exceed $30,000 per year.

381) Baby Sitting Service- For a babysitting service you would charge a flat rate of $17 per hour, the baby sitting service could generate profits of $50,000 per year. Carefully screen sitters make sure their trustworthy and reliable.

382) Weekend Courier Service- To start this service, simply contracts your courier service to established courier companies on a as needed basis, The more profitable way would be to establish weekend delivery contracts with local merchants and professionals. You will need reliable transportation, as well as a beeper or cell phone for incoming inquiries.

383) Commercial Event Planner- A commercial event planner put together seminars, trade shows, conferences, corporate parties and special events and activities. The focus on these events would be raising public awareness, training employees, boosting morale, and encouraging teamwork. You must be well organized to carry these duties out.

384) Party and Wedding Planner- Bar Mitzvahs, weddings, anniversaries, and many more other personal occasions that need planning guidance, this can be a fun business for someone well organized. Your client list will be your greatest asset, the job would be clearly more than putting the pieces together, it means being a great listener and getting very involved. You'll also need to immerse yourself in what can possibly be done at weddings and parties of all types. Wedding expense often exceeds in the range of $40,000 and a Bar Mitzvah can exceed as much as $25,000

385) Ceiling Cleaning Service- Start a ceiling cleaning service can be expensive or not, simply purchase a few buckets, a swivel head cleaning pad, and a ladder and don't forget to get liability insurance. A basic marketing campaign can consist of flier distribution and introductory telephone calls build an alliance with commercial property managers, firms and offices, ceiling cleaning profits are excellent for this type of service.

386) Garage and Estate Sale Promoter- If you possess good marketing and organizational skill you can start a business that hot garage and estate sales, your duties will include, displaying, organizing, and selling items, and clean up after the sale is over. To secure future business simply hand out promotional brochures and tell the people attending about your service.

387) Small Engine Repair- Small engine repair services repair lawn mowers, chain saws, this kind of business can be very lucrative. An additional business income can be generated by providing your clients with optional services such as saw, blades sharpening, as well as small equipment rentals.

388) Personal Shopper- Personal shoppers have a passion for shopping; you can extend your services to people who are not able to get out such as seniors. Well placed ad's on your website will help you market yourself and your services, you can also hand out business cards to seniors in retirement homes the profits for a business like this are excellent.

389) Escort Service-Escort services are a legitimate way for people to hook up for dinner dates, a movie, parties, you would need to screen all you escorts very carefully, You must let it be known to local law enforcement ad your clients and potential clients that your escort service is legit. You can charge clients 4200 and up per hour for your services and split the profits with your escorts.

390) Party Dj Service- A DJ service commands anywhere from 42,000 to $7,000 for parties, weddings, and $4,000 for Bar Mitzvahs, this could be your ticket to wealth if you have the dj ability and skills

391) Personal Trainer- The key to success with being a personal trainer is knowing the right program for your clients by accessing their needs, you could build your business by word of mouth along with some basis advertisements. If you're considering starting such a business, you're earning could be $40K to $50k and if you decide to sell health related products and earning could be even more.

392) Image Consultant- An image consultant work with individuals and corporate clients on developing the best image for success, you will also consult your clients on communication skills and behavior the earnings are great for this type of business. As discussed in full in the beginning of the book.

393) Ticket Broker- you could legally break tickets for sports events, theater, concerts, establish contact with stadiums, and purchase blocks of tickets, or be on the list to sell tickets on consignment, market your ticket business for tourist, hotels, and also try to align yourself with corporate clients.

394) Personal Assistant- Corporate executive and business owners all utilize the services of a personal assistant. Duties performed by a personal assistant includes everything from booking appointments, to returning business phone calls, in some cases picking dry cleaning, to buying gifts for friends and family of your clients, you must have computer skills, and traveling is a must when working as a personal assistant.

395) Temp Help Agency- Starting a home base temp agency is a great business venture, you job would be to recruit workers prepared to work on a temporary basis By creating an informational package describing your services and workforce, and distribute the package to businesses and companies that occasionally rely on temporary workers your business will grow from this point and profit potential is wonderful.

396) Running Distress Sales- A distress sale is based on items that a person need, by scanning your local classified ads, or collecting advertisements and products for sale that interest you, and wait at least four weeks, once the four weeks are up call the owners of the product to see if they're ready to sell, you should have no problem getting the items for the price you

propose, if so, offer a low ball offer, you must be a strong negotiator.

397) Home Gym Designer- Your duties would be to transform existing rooms into home gyms, establish a price formula for the business. Start up cost should be around $9,500 to establish this business, and maintain yearly sales of $200,000 this would result in gross profits of $66,000

398) Used Golf Balls- Secure contracts with public and private golf courses, your duties would be to retrieve golf balls from the water and other hazards on and around the golf course, if you retrieve golf balls that has been used by celebrity golf tournaments and have the name of the tournament stamped on it, you could as much as $25 or more per ball, a ball that has a celebrities name on it is worth as much as $500

399) Fitness Classes for Dogs and Their Owners-This is a unique business opportunity, The classes should be conducted outside and should be designed with dogs and their owners in mind, Profit potentials are great a mere 20 students pay $5 per day for one hour classes will create a $50 profit for you, for a class like this advertising can be by word of mouth.

400) Fitness Center- This is a very profitable business opportunity Opening this type of center takes careful planning, and research. And the following aspect of the business should be considered location, operating format, staff, wages, marketing, safety, competition; this is a huge business undertaking and should be researched carefully.

401) Children Only Fitness Classes-Conducting a children's only fitness class should be categorized by the children's age groups, for beginner though advanced age, research prior to starting a children's only fitness business includes operating location, required certification, health and safety regulations, and of course liability insurance.

402) Bicycle Repair Service- A bicycle repair service is a great business venture this can be a home base business, with low startup capital, a proven consumer demand, you could generate earnings of $40 per our as a full time , part time opportunity only thing you'll need is repair skill.

403) Pitch and Putt Golf- Pitch and putt course are generally 18 holes ranging from 50 to 100 yards each Good golfers have the opportunity to practice their short game, you will need to stock up on nine irons, pitching wedges, putters, and scorecards, you can also add 9 holes for a generous package rate.

404) Coaching Service- whether you're coaching one on one or helping a young athlete there is a growing need for athletic coaches, Coaches can run clinic with their sports expertise, and you can start a business like this from home with a solid marketing plan includes reaching out to students, and local leagues, and sports clubs.

405) Hand Car Wash-For an investment of less than $10,000 you can open your own hand wash, car wash, strike up a deal with gas stations, merchant garages, and car dealers, to set up car washing in a section of their parking lots, you will need a small shed for equipment storage and a 10 by 20 foot tent to wash cars under, if you wash 20 cars per day charging $10 each you could generate an income of $6,000 per month.

406) Mobile Car Wash- You could start a mobile car wash for less than $10,000 you could also generate an income of $60,000 there is no skill required, you could also run this business from a home base, the business only requires basic equipment.

407) Used Car Sales- You'll need a car selling permit, you'll also need a good location with great street visibility and an initial inventory of cars to sell, you can start a website the income potential for this venture is excellent.

408) Auto Towing- you must obtain a license to operate or start an auto towing business, towing licenses are heavily regulated. With a business like this it may be hard to secure proper liability insurance, purchasing a towing license and a truck can cost as much as $200,000 with no towing account in place.

409) Car Finder's Service- As the owner of a car finder's serviced you would find particular types of car's for your clients RV, trucks, vans, cars, revenues are generated by negotiating a commission for your services, You can easily generate an income of $50,000 per year

410) Mobile Oil Change Service- For a business of this nature a mechanical license is not required to perform oil changes, just about anyone can do this, your only duties would be to supply your customers with exceptional service, Once established a mobile oil change service can provide the owner of the business with a good yearly income.

411) Automotive Maintenance Guide- If you have sales and marketing skills, excellent profits can be earned by creating and distributing an auto maintenance guide that can be published every spring and fall of each year. Once established the profit potential can range from $20,000 per year.

412) Motorcycle Sales- To sell second hand motorcycles you could operate from a home base provided you have the proper zoning requirements, you could also operate your business from a small rental location, all you'll need to do is practice good research and negotiation skills, if you achieve annual sales of $20,000 will result in an income of $70,000

413) Paint Touch up Service- To start an automotive touch up service, the paint you'll need is supplied by most automotive supply stores, you can operate this business from a truck, van, or even a trailer, but in order to carry out this sort of business you must have the skills you'll need to be a success. The current rate for this kind of service is $50 for a basic scratch to paint and buff; you can go as high as $200 for more different paint touch up jobs.

414) Sunroof Installation- You can operate this business as a home base business installing if your business also provides a mobile installation service, be sure to establish alliances with car dealers in the local community, pop open automotive sunroofs.

415) Airport Shuttle Service-You must obtain an operator's license for this business venture. An airport shuttle service can be a very profitable business to own and operate. You can market your service at hotels, major airports, and travel agencies.

416) Mobile Refuel Service-This business will take a large investment to establish as much as $100,000, however the truck and other required equipment could be leased. Your main customers for this type of service or unique business will be contractors with heavy earth moving machinery, machinery that is thirsty for fuel. There are very strict regulations in this industry; the key to success is to be on call and ready to refuel equipment 7 days a week.

417) Children's Coach Service- This is a taxi service that specializes in moving kid' s from point A to point B, you will need a taxi or limo license and permits to get this business going. But once you have the necessary licensing you will need to demonstrate exemplary driving skills and be extremely reliable.

418) Car Rental- A car rental service that rent exotic cars, and rent only certain motorcycles like Harley s, and specialized convertible cars , this is a niche market. To have a successful business, you would need to establish an alliance with hotels, business associations, and corporations and businesses. You'll also need liability insurance; the profits will come from being innovative, just as long as you provide great customer service.

419) Bicycle Taxi Service- This is what we call a Pedi-cab service, once established licensing have been obtained you can be well on your way while peddling your way to profits. There are many styles of Pedi cabs ranging from two to six occupants, and the

cost of purchasing a Pedi cab $3,500, but ride or rental rates are 8 to 10 per fifteen minutes with a minimum $5 charge this is a great business venture.

420) Horse and Buggy Ride- This can be a simple and profitable business venture, the start-up is simple. You'll need to check local licensing and permits to operate this type of service; you'll also need several horses and a buggy which can cost $1,000 to $10,000 depending on the horse. Horse and buggy rides can start at $15 per person or go up to $150 per couple package.

421) Off Road Tours- Off road tours are usually an all day or half day package, Clients are currently priced $50 to $150 per person. Advertising and promoting off road tours or backwoods tours is very easy, this kind of business can be very profitable.

422) Bicycle Tours- The key to success in a bicycle tour business is that your tours would have to be unique, fun, and interesting and should be organized around a central theme. Promoting and advertising the business in all media, websites and also list your bicycle tours with travel agencies and brokers, Start up cost is as much as $20,000 to $72,000 currently hourly rates range from $50 to $70 per person per day, for a full day $75 to $125. Profit potential range is $20,000 per year, part time, $40,000 per year full time.

423) Travel Kits- Starting a business that produce and distribute specialty travel kits could put you on the path to financial freedom. The kits could contain items such as maps, language dictionaries, attraction and tour discount coupons, mini first aid kits and toothbrushes. You could sell these kits directly to travel agents and brokers on a wholesale basis, or directly to consumers via a website.

424) Bed and Breakfast Guide- A bed and breakfast is a great business venture and a great way to meet new people, Typically a B&B stay would range from $30 to $100 per night per person including breakfast. You could promote your B&B by joining travel and tourism associations, and enlisting it in a online directory. You will also need liability insurance and meet local fire and safety, building codes, and zoning ordinances.

425) Teen Travel Tours- To start this business, you will need to put together a travel package with young teens in mind. Activities, meals, lodging, utilize a combination of dorms, camping, and hotels. A 2 to 6 week summer package can sell anywhere from $2,000 to $9,000 and this can be a home based business also.

426) Senior Tours- If you start a senior tour service you would have to put together an itinerary for each tour package that cater to the needs of seniors. Research before putting this package together, the key to success contacts and the packages you offer. This should include air transportation, hotels, guide

tours, meals, ground transportation's, and other accommodations you can make this a profitable business venture.

427) Online Travel Games for Kid's- You can create game phrases, stories, songs, rhymes, or other activities for kids. There are several options when marketing travel games; you can create a book of original games, or some classic travel favorites, however you decide to create the travel games just make sure you market your business to all kid friendly locations as well as travel agencies and all travel online websites.

428) Online Coloring Books- If you create websites with downloadable pictures, images, animals, buildings, landscapes all in print form, children can use a printer to print and color these images with crayons, you can sell ad's or have sponsors for this site for extra income.

429) Online Star Search- A website the enables wanna be movie stars, singers, and performers, to have a chance at fame. People with talent can submit digital footage of their performance, then vote for the best performer. This is a unique online venture. This could also provide an outstanding opportunity to generate revenue by renting advertising space on your site.

430) Online Entertainment Coupons- Design a website that is indexed by various entertainment services and products such as concerts, plays, movies, and the theater, secure companies and businesses within the entertainment industry to advertise discounts, apply to their specific products and devices. Provide new coupons from a vendor every week of even every day

431) Online Entertainment Listings and Reviews- Set up a series of local websites proving area listening and reviews, your movie reviews can be posted on all the sites, the sites can also list entertainment reviews section with feedback. Your site can earn income by selling ad space to local merchants in each area, or by film companies would also advertise.

432) Online Movie Set Location- Starting a movie set location rental business will make you a cyber scout, you can establish a website with various categories for filming locations, these categories could include factories, vacant lots, and land, unique houses, office buildings, to make this work you would need to scout a number of unique sites, profit potential is outstanding

433) Online Movie Trivia- You could start a movie trivia site that focuses on movie trivia for all ages, as well as horror, action, and comedy; these can also be a part of your site. You could even list games and contest and sell microwave popcorn.

434) Online Games Site- Immerse yourself in the gaming world that's if you want to set up a gaming site so that you can determine which games you want to present to your site clients. If your site promotes other peoples games you can provide previews and reviews and trivia versions.

435) Online Fantasy Sport Site-Setting up a site that handles statistical aspects of fantasy leagues, can be quite profitable, The league pays you per team fee to provide the league with their own pages, to each team as well as central pages for transactions, league news, free agent etc... Once you have established your site you can rake in the bucks.

436) Online Board Games- Chess, Backgammon, Chinese checkers, checkers, the website would allow them to play games against opponents in other parts of the country. To start you'll need to visit and study the existing game sites to see how you can make such a site work smoothly so that visitors can enjoy the opportunity to play games and you can profit from this.

437) Online Children Stories- Post great children's writers' stories on a children's story website, with permission you can post stories from published children's book authors, parents can sign up, pay a monthly membership fee, make sure you have a fairly large selection of at least 50 stories and keep posting new ones every month.

438) Online Theater Directory- This kind of site post movies, and theater, plays, musicals, your job would be to find the theater, including traveling one and children theater groups, the fee for a more detailed listening could add up to a good annual income for you, you could also post reviews.

439) Online Art Print- Design a website that exclusively features art prints for sale, the artist would ship it to the purchaser and would receive a percentage of the sales value, this cyber venture is easy to establish and you could generate from a home base.

440) Online Wooden Toys- Your website would include all types of wooden toys and games constructed by numerous individuals and small manufacturing firms, you have two options in terms of earning income, First you could create an online, wooden toy store and charge a commission on all sales generated, the second would be to establish a website in a directory format and charge toy makers to be listed.

441) Online Collectible Clothing- You could start a website the features online exclusive collectible clothing or an online classified service. You could generate revenue and profit, including charging a fee to list items for sale, renting banners and adverting space, buying collectible clothing, reselling them yourself via the website for profit.

442) Online Blue Jeans- Start a website that offers custom made to order blue jeans. Feature the capabilities of letting visitors design their own blue jeans, all your visitors will have to do is enter their measurements, inseam length, waist size, cuff diameter, and they would simply submit and wait for the jeans to arrive what better way to make a living

443) Online Lingerie Shop- To start an online lingerie shop you would need to secure wholesalers purchase accounts, with the lingerie designers and manufactures. Design an easy to navigate website featuring lingerie for sale, post photos of models wearing your product on the site, establish accredit card ordering system, and package and ship program to fill your orders, you can market your business through links, offline advertising, and lingerie parties and fashion shows.

444) Online Fabric Shop- Develop a portal that brings fashion designer and fabric designers together, you could earn revenues by charging them both, fabric manufacturers and retailers a fee to use your directory site. Potential customers would be hobby seamstress, fashion designers, interior decorators, tailors, advertise to all remote communities that don't have fabric shops.

445) Online Software- staring this type of online business, you would need to secure an agreement with software developers, and represent and market their products. A direct mail and email marketing campaign aimed at the industry or individuals

that you're trying to reach, promote by registering search engines, linking to topics related sites, utilize chat rooms keep limited inventory and provide good customer service.

446)) Online Sportswear- To start a sportswear line online just purchase your inventory on a wholesale basis, via the internet, along with home selling parties, provide a wide range of brands, sizes, styles, or you could establish a business that design and manufacture sportswear to be sold directly to consumers via the internet. Just make sure to get a patent on any original designs.

447) Online Art Auction- Amateur artist is seeking a way to sell their work, this creates an opportunity to start an online auction service, consider building an alliance with major players on the website, revenues and profits will be created when artwork has been successfully auctioned, retain a commission of 10 to 25 % of the total sales for services provided.

448) Online Art Gallery- online art gallery offer work of art for sale, the artist featured on the site pay a monthly fee and commission upon the successful sale of art. The key to success rely on promoting and marketing the site. Also ask the artist if you can display their work in restaurants and other locations which can help them sell their work.

449) Online Craft Supply Sales- You can develop a website that features craft supplies of every sort for sale, you could also run displays advertisements in craft magazines and kick off a direct mail campaign aimed specifically at people in the art and craft industry, you could set up sites so that people buy directly from you and the orders shipped directly from suppliers, revenues would be generated by charging manufactures and distributions a fee for listing and being featured on your website.

450) Online Craft Show- You can start your own virtual online craft show year round, producing crafts on a full or part time basis, you will need a marketing and distributor outlet and this is it. The site can include registering, with search engines, traditional print mediums, like magazines, craft newsletters, and all types of publications. Develop ad publishing this type of website will require substantial development and marketing budget.

451) Online Farmers Market- Create an online farmers market by developing site that features farm fresh products for sale, this site would be marketed to restaurant owners and consumers buying $50 and up worth of fresh products, the profit potential at outstanding from this type of business.

452) Online Seafood Sales- Take seafood sales and delivery online and open your business to consumers all year round, develop your own website that features seafood, select the seafood the customers want to order, select payment and shipping information and wait for delivery. This concept will require a great amount of planning, but the profit potential is there.

453) Online Organic Food Sales- This is a good time to start a online business that specialize in organic foods, you would need to establish an alliance with organic food growers to supply the inventory you'll need. Make sure your customers will be able to place orders online, the profit potential for a business like this sells and delivers organic grown fruits and veggies is outstanding.

454) Online Birdhouse Sale- You could sell birdhouses online, sell your birdhouse creation from your site, market and promote via internet advertising. Birdhouses built from all over the world. People could have their birdhouses listed on your site for a flat fee or commission for this service

455) Online Comic Book Sales- You could start a business that buy and sale rare comic books via online develop a website so that anyone could post or list their comics on your site for sale, Once the book sold you would collect a 10 to 20% commission . You could easily generate a full time income.

456) Online Golf Information and Equipment-You could start an online business that caters to golf fanatics, this could make you very rich, create and seek a niche, a golfers coupon site wherein visitors could locate deals online, and online golf instruction, if you combine these ideas you will definitely will have it made.

457) Online Fencing Equipment- If you can find low cost fencing equipment for student in college taking fencing classes, you could be on your way to a very successful business. You will need to market your products to fencing clubs, supply your clients with a chat room on your website; this could make your site a home for those who love fencing.

458) Online Used Motorcycle Parts- Start a business that stock and sell second hand used motorcycle parts. The parts can be inexpensive when you purchase motorcycles from insurance companies that have been written off due to damage or theft

459) Online Advertising Broker- Develop a website then let small business owners and professionals list the type of advertising they are seeking, and the price they are prepared to pay. This type of website would require careful planning, but the profit potentials are outstanding.

460) Online Lotteries- Develop a website the features and provides site visitors with news and information pertaining to lotteries from around the world, this could provide to be a very lucrative and profitable website. Electronic winning numbers forecast and information on how to purchase tickets, stories about hitting it big, just make sure to research all legal aspects of the business before posting.

461) Online Baby Name Directory- Baby name books have always been popular, perhaps you could create a website with historical baby names, and their meanings, or perhaps you could create a website with celebrity baby names, and how they came to be changed or altered to suit their personality's. Visitors could browse through the names for free, and you could rent, advertising space or sell products to businesses looking to reach soon to be parents.

462) Online E- Newsletters- The key to this website getting e-news letters to customers online, just make sure the contents is good enough to keep people coming back every week. Maintaining a client's news letter should require no more than 6 to 10 hours of work per month. Aim to secure 15 regular customers paying a mere $300 each per month for the service which is only $3,000 per year to keep your product in front of customers.

463) Online E-log Design-Designing corporate and product logos for free has the potential to earn you $30,000 or more per year. Surf the web for corporate product logos that could be improved or for companies and products; use your design skills and basic computer hardware and design new logos for the same corporations, a few logo sales can result in big money.

464) Online Business Plan- You can market an online service to new business owners and future entrepreneurs and make a nice profit selling the templates for $100 each. You can offer expert advice for free, and you could provide a valuable service, you can also sell business plan books though the site to make more money.

465) Online Actor Directory- Posting an actor's online directory might just make you a financial star, you can charge actors and models a small yearly fee, to post their headshots and resumes on the site, directors, casting agents, and producers would only be a click away.

466) Online Loans- An online loan delivery can feature business start up home improvement and automotive loans or all types, and all types of financial services. Bankers, venture capitalist, and other lending institutions, would pay a yearly fee to be listed on the site, the idea is to market the site as a place they can shop around for a loan.

467) Online Vending Equipment-Develop a website the specializes in providing a one stop source for vending information and details, market the site to the general public placing small classified ads in major newspapers under the business opportunity section, also market the site to business publications and links, to websites that focus on this kind of business.

468) Online Home Repair and Improvement- Utilize your construction and renovation expertise by developing a website that features all sorts of advice and information on home improvement on home repairs the site could include industry and news about products, questions and answers from people working on home improvement projects. Just make sure you include some home repair tips to generate return visitors to your site.

469) Online Dog Training- A dog training website could provide visitors with everything they want to know about dogs, a directory of dog trainers from coast to coast, digital video broadcasting, articles and information generated income by selling ad space on the site, and by selling dog training programs , books, and videos.

470) Online Dog Care Website- Develop a website that can bring dog lovers together, you could feature all kinds of products, service and information. You could include articles written by vets, and by dog owners, a chat room could be included, a pet

survey and quizzes and even an e card with pouch pictures. Te income potential is earned by charging retailers and service provider a fee for featuring their listings.

471) Online Mortgage Broker- An online mortgage broker this is a niche market in order to succeed and profit you would need to build a directory of mortgage brokers that specialize in high risk, property financing, create a portal that brings provide investors together feature mortgage brokers that lend exclusively for second and third mortgage financing. Your revenues will generate by charging listing fees and selling ad space.

472) Online Parking Space Directory- This site could post listening of garages with availability along with individuals who have space in garages, your site could also provide parking rules and regulations. For various towns and cities, and major cities, you should also have special sections for special event parking.

473) Online Resort Directory- Develop a site that lists all sorts of unique resorts around the world, and list what make them unique. The key is finding reputable sources that could give you the thumbs up or down. Categorize resorts for golf, families, seniors, honeymooners, promote you sit-in all travel publications and by linking to travel websites.

474) Online Hot Air Balloon Directory- Start a business that sells and promote hot air balloon tours, the business can operate as a booking agency for balloon tours, and operate from around the world. Once customers have booked a balloon tour a commission of 25% would be charged on the total value, this site can also provide clients with options to book helicopter or small planes for sightseeing.

475) Online Press Release Service-A website that allows clients to log on and create press releases from the many templates available, you could also include writing editing and consultation services. Activate and service like this would require countless hours of dedication, researching formatting do the research of you want to make this work.

476) Online American History- To set up this type of website you must research to make sure your information is accurate, you could bring in teachers, and other education professionals to help create and build up the website and its contents. Selling history books, maps, and other historical products would provide you with a hefty income.

477) Online Casino Directory- why not create a website that features casino reviews, a list of all the top casinos, supply visitors with special casino promotions, online contest polls, and other activities.

478) Online Beach Directory- You could develop a website that categorizes beaches by location. Directory, charging facilities, parking prices, food availability, phone call centers, and the facility can also provide email and fax locations for business owners on vacation. Also list special events and activities generate income by selling beach friendly products.

479) Online National Park Directory- You could set up a website that provides detailed information on each of the nation national parks, this can feature directories, accommodations, where to eat, campgrounds, and the history of each park. You could also set up chat rooms, posting broads and market the site at tourist bureaus and sporting goods and camping supplies locations.

480) Online Real Estate website Consultant- To set this website up you do not need to be an expert in real estate just study some of the basics. You can charge 440 to $60 an hour to make a site like this you must be up to date with your data.

481) Online Studio Directory- This type of site can generate income from detailed directory listening as well as advertisements and you can do a specialized search for members to find them the size studio and right location they're looking for, market this site to dance studio instructors, film makers, independent producers, and advertising executives.

482) Online Toys and games- You could profit from an eBay business selling the latest toys and games, you can also do very well selling older toys. Research the market and decide where you fit in

483) Jewelry and Watches- You could profit from selling jewelry and watches, you could bid with profit in mind keep a wide variety of watches in stock, since style and taste vary these are great items on eBay.

484) True Crime Writer- Murderous tales of love, and stories about the strangest, stupidest twisted crimes, Writing stories about true crime can earn you a great living. You could write on a freelance basis or you could write a novel. Potential purchase of the articles includes newspapers, magazines and short stories publishers.

485) Editing Service- An editing service is not limited to publishers, and book authors or potential clients can also include advertising agencies, marketing agencies, web content directors, actually just about any company, organization, or individual that need to ensure that print or electronic information is spelled correctly that the grammar is correct, potential income range $5 to $50 per hour for your service.

486) Letter Writing Service-Many people, including business owners, politicians, students, an job seekers are more than

willing to part with a few dollars to obtain a well written letter that clearly express their intent and purpose, your income potential can range from $20 to $30 per hour.

487) Children Story Writer- writing children's stories can be extremely profitable; this industry demands unique and fresh stories constantly. You would need to find commercial publishers prepared to take on and publish your story. Or you could self publish.

488) Trivia Writer- Researching and writing about fun trivia can be fun; you could write trivia for magazines, by marketing your trivia questions and information to suit the genre of the publication. The trick is to turn out fresh material on a regular basis.

489) Literary Agent- You could earn a six figure income as a literary agent, all you'll have to do is get the clients you represent to agree that you will receive a 10 to 20% commission on all work that is successfully sold to a publisher, including television and movie rights.

490) Creative Mailing List- Profit potential is $25,000 to $100,000 mailing list sell for as much as per name here lies an exciting business opportunity, you must have great marketing skill and a computer, your mailing list should be compiled by industry and target market.

491) Where They Are Now Book- Celebrity, politician, entertainers, or just everyday people written in you where they are now books, there are two options for publishing and distributing this type of book, establish commercial publisher or self publish. Just make sure that you create a new twist in terms of the internet storyline or type of people.

492) Speech Writer- Speech writing is an art form, creative writing flair, excellent research and communication skills can be generated a great income, in order to make it in this business you need to excel at writing speeches. Just prepare a few sample speeches on various subjects and distribute to potential clients, corporate executive, leaders in local associations, and politicians. Once established this business can, personally, and financially grow.

493) Family Tree Research- Family tree research is a service that connect you with your family members, people have an interest in finding out more about their family tree income potential range from $20 to $40 per hour.

494) Who's Who Directory- A who's who directory features people from your local community, this book is nothing more than a listing of people that includes detailed information on them, this is really used for the purpose of hiring individuals for their skill in certain areas, you profit can be very good from this type of business venture.

495) Self Help Writer - Once you know your area of expertise you can sell self help books and guides on the subjects. People purchase this type of book because they want to improve some aspect of their lives or want to learn how to do something better.

496) Business Plan Writer- if you have the skill of examining a business idea in detail and can put together that idea on paper in the right format, and with a necessary support material you can have a successful home based business. People would rather an expert rather than a software package when dealing with something this significant.

497) Copy Write Service- You can start a business like this by approaching all sorts of business as well as ad agencies and websites with a portfolio of diversified samples demonstrating your skills, once you have dazzled your clients put together a price brochure and a website you can charge $700 and up for direct mail packages.

498) Technical Writer- Technical writing can range from material for websites, to instruct, and manuals, to documentation by anything from news, to medical technology, to video games market your abilities to manufacturing companies. You must be an expert in all things technical and have good communication skills.

499) Ghostwriting Service- Ghostwriters turn the words and ideas of clients in a readable manuscript, if you have a gift for making other people sound good you can be a highly sort after ghostwriter. Post your own website and get in contact with literary agents and publishers who can send you clients.

500) Professional Reader- Readers are hired to read manuscripts, publishing houses, agents, will give you a parameter within which to base your write ups on so that you can provide them with an accurate overview of the manuscript in conjunction with their needs, you can market yourself to literary agents, and or publishers you'll need to be able to read fast, make concise informed decisions about different manuscripts.